Tell Them I Said No

Tell Them I Said No

Martin Herbert

Sternberg Press

For Eva

The house is smoky, and I quit it.
—Marcus Aurelius, *Meditations*

Introduction

They make me feel dirty and inadequate, those websites—the ones featuring couples and groups, tides of bodies, old and young. You've probably looked at the photographs too, taken at openings and dinners and parties, artists with arms slung eagerly around dealers and collectors, grinning for the flash, available, biddable, ugh. But still I look—in the past I even supplied content—and when I look, I sometimes think of Stanley, who's never there. Of Stanley, Albert, Cady, David, Laurie, and others, past and present habitués of the opposite of "there."

The photographs I possess of Stanley Brouwn make me feel dirty as well. The artist, who since the early 1970s has snubbed almost every form of publicity, tried to destroy all trace of them. But people, especially when they've been commanded otherwise, will talk and show, and others will listen and look and take smartphone snaps of those photos they can't keep. Faced with a muteness as artful in its chicanery, as paradoxically gifting as Brouwn's turns out to be, one might twist between appreciating the nimbus of silence around a practice and, teased and goaded, commissioning scratch translations of sneakily recorded phone interviews with him found on YouTube. The following essays twist. Distancing is a leaky boat, increasingly so.

Nevertheless, such self-detaching on the part of artists goes somewhere. As performed today, it pushes against the current in an epoch of celebrity worship and its related feedback loop, increasingly universal visibility and access. A big part of the artist's role now, in a massively professionalized art world, is showing up to self-market, being *present*. On all channels, ideally: see how, aside from all the photo opportunities, far-from-digital-native figures take to social media or splash themselves when possible across magazines (which grander galleries now produce themselves) or collaborate with fashion designers, all gates open.[1] For younger artists, meanwhile, the visible crown of youth can seem like a necessary attribute. The paradigmatic figure might be the art student too busy with exhibitions and networking prospects to graduate, flanked by flippers, a five-year career ahead of them.

In such a context of hectic short-termism and multiple types of over-sharing, some kind of voluntary retreat, some respect for the Joycean triumvirate of silence, exile, and cunning, might constitute a vanguard, if a difficult and apparently suicidal one to countenance today since it seemingly requires earning the right to leave. (And an increasingly rare forbearance on the part of one's gallerist.) But for a range of artists, particularly over the last half-century—since the ascendance of Pop and the idea of the artist as celebrity prototyped by Dalí and, more quietly, Gauguin, perfected by Warhol, and updated by Koons, Hirst, and so on—positioning oneself somewhere on the axis of absenting has served, variously, as a reservoir of energy and a permission for idiosyncrasy and, trite as it sounds, inner journeying. It has constituted, among other things, a hardscrabble route toward integrity where the tail doesn't wag the dog, a cipher of self-actualization, a symbolic resistance to gendered or racial subjection, a species of performance, and a seductive projection screen predicated on the theory that the more someone runs away, the more we'll run after them. None of this, meanwhile, has transpired in a steady-state art world.[2] Rather, the urge to pull back, where felt, echoes changing conditions over decades, from the swing toward dematerialization and its intersection with critique, to art's transmogrification into a backcloth for the power plays of the prosperous.[3]

Marcel Duchamp, who claimed to have traded art for chess but toiled in secret for two decades on his *Étant donnés* (1946–66), and who told Calvin Tomkins in 1964 that he thought "the great man of tomorrow in the way of art cannot be seen, should not be seen, and should go underground,"[4] is the public face of this standoffish school, so patently that there's no essay-length footnote here to his art's endlessly foaming exegesis.[5] If a handful of other figures have followed the self-described "breather" in being at once inside and outside the art system, perhaps the most remarkable is David Hammons, who treats the art world as a high-stakes game of strategy to be played from a highly critical distance. Hammons doesn't come to us. We come to him, effectively at his bidding. Another of his progenitors, Yves Klein, wrote a judo manual[6]—in art and in martial arts, its author pursued judo's precept of "the minimum effort for the maximum effectiveness"—and one might see in all the aforementioned tacticians' practice a technique of using the art world's weight against it. That's the case for Stanley Brouwn, for Lutz Bacher, and for a figure such as Maurizio Cattelan, who at the time of writing may have retired or may have not.

Some artists withdraw temporarily, out of necessity. In 2007 I asked Robert Gober what he planned to do next—he was just about to mount a major mid-career retrospective, the kind of sketch for a tombstone that can paralyze an artist—and he said he intended to let his assistants go and really not do much for the next five years except retrench and reconsider. This struck me as fully admirable, though somewhat unlikely. It turned out to be more or less true.

Sometimes there's no choice: that appears to have been the case for Agnes Martin. And sometimes when there's no choice, depending on the reason, absconding manifests as total, tools-down nonparticipation. Exemplified here by Charlotte Posenenske, Cady Noland, and Laurie Parsons, this is the far end of the continuum of remove this book sketches out. Full withdrawal registers as exasperated reaction to the intolerability of the art world, to the limits of political potential, to gender bias, profiteering, the presence of repellent personalities, and neon egos. The structural sexism of this sphere may, as the examples named above already suggest, underwrite one broad cleaving along gender lines among these practices—that men are more likely to step back to a safe distance and women to quit outright. Precisely why this might be—beyond the wearying perpetuation of disparity in prices, representation in museums, and so on—is something I've tried to address on a case-by-case basis. Research also suggests, though, that the official narratives aren't always fully accurate: that while history implies certain artists walked out and slammed the door, in reality they opened it again, or sought to, or never quite closed it.

We sustain the approved story line sometimes out of unawareness, sometimes for sentimental reasons. In the latter cases, voluntarily or not, the refusenik operates as—to use the epithet Christine Mehring once applied to Posenenske—our "bad conscience." We project our own misgivings about the art world upon such a figure; upraise their rep as a gutsy ideal.

(Some writings about Noland read like love letters.) Wholly quitting or making oneself inaccessible can also be a deliberate conceptual act. Witness Tehching Hsieh's work. Following a series of endurance performances and a long period in which he said he would make art but not show it (in the end, his work boiled down to a single terse statement: "I kept myself alive"), the Taiwanese artist officially quit art in 2000; he has kept his word. Or witness, as essayed in this book, Christopher D'Arcangelo's practice, in which withdrawal takes its darkest and most irreversible turn. Even when not framed as such, though, a partial disaffiliating can tempt one to register it as a para-artwork in its own right—the degree to which that is truly the case is something wrestled with, where appropriate, in the essays that follow—and creates its own momentum. The sway of such gestures is testified to by exploits like the samizdat exhibitions, in which Hammons's and Noland's works were "recreated from images found on the internet and in exhibition catalogues," organized by New York curatorial outfit Triple Candie in 2006. Full-on quitters like Noland, "dropout artists" as some have termed them, are naturally objects of particular fascination, not to say romanticism and vicariousness.[7] Even if their acts are the reactive results of extreme vexation, they illuminate a road not traveled by others who might wish they dared. They also constitute an example of what's possible, articulated in the negative, when you're not terrified by the attention economy.

There is a shadow history here, too: that of those artists who drift out of the art world all the time, flouting the pious assumption that one must always remain in it, because—well, actually, *why* exactly? The more unassuming leavers' names are lost to history. A decade ago I met a spectrally calm young man who made limpid paintings of consumer objects, items of worldly contemplation underwritten by their maker's meditation practice. He told me his surname was a pseudonym, though it was only years later that I realized he'd taken it from that of a Zen monk recluse, and by that time—after a career of five years, tops—he'd completely vanished, gone from galleries, the Internet (mostly), everything. A Pyrrhic victory, perhaps, but also a reminder that the art world isn't everything and an art career doesn't have to last a lifetime. We can probably all name artists who don't quit but should.

Concerning those who don't leave, what one longs for—or what this writer, who sees too many exhibitions that are blatantly products of the studio treadmill, which circularly pay for the assistants and the fair-booth acreage, longs for—is some tactical thinking. No artist needs to undertake a half-dozen solo shows per year, plus fairs, plus a continual side salad of group shows. Artists who do this, given the unassailable fact that most of them are not modern-day Picassos, will in most cases burn out and deliver diminishing returns in the meantime. One wishes, however vainly—one writes, at least in part, to accrue useful examples of such—for artists to make statements when necessary and to be silent when not.[8] We have no shortage of art, or of galleries, and, as Mark Twain once said, "No word was ever as effective as a rightly timed pause."

The art business runs on personalities, at least in part, and personalities can be powerfully elliptical too. Not least because surprise, in an era of artistic production lines determined by the frequency of fairs, is a rare property in art. Among younger artists one might look to someone like Trisha Donnelly, not removed from the art world per se but refusing interviews and presenting exhibitions increasingly without elucidatory supports, as someone who has exemplarily figured out the weight and value of silence and self-containment. A figure like Bacher who prefigures her, meanwhile, has for many years operated less like most artists than like, say, Scott Walker, whose musical career over the last three decades has been a string of well-timed pauses punctuated by out-of-the-blue statements crafted on his own terms, and whose visual iconography these days reduces to a baseball cap hiding his eyes.

❀

I bought an issue of *Pop*, partly because I wanted to read the Grimes interview and partly because I was amused by a strapline on the cover, trailing an artist's Instagram artworks ("♥ Richard Prince ♥ so jazzed about the new era!!!"). Then I went back to thinking about Albert York—a rare retrospective of his paintings had just gone up at Matthew Marks, New York, at the same time as Richard Prince's contentious social media–derived works were hanging at Gagosian Gallery. A couple of painter friends who stay in a lot had alerted me to York a few years before. His story has been rehearsed a few times, most famously by Tomkins in a 1995 *New Yorker* profile. It's a tale of steady, determined secession that echoes Balzac's short story of artistic frustration, "The Unknown Masterpiece" (1831) — moving away from New York, sending his paintings to his gallerist wrapped in brown paper, refusing retrospectives, impossible standards leaving York feeling, so he told Tomkins, that almost all he'd done was bad — going round and round in an increasingly small place but seeing it with an intensity that's almost violent. The paintings he made between the mid-1960s and early '80s convey that: still lifes and paintings of cows and landscapes and the occasional surreal Native American that stage a transfiguring of reality — trees appear sentient amid gilded moonlight, cut flowers come across as gigantic, architectonic things — which language, or at least mine, doesn't get very close to.

York was, by all accounts, chronically shy, but he turned that around, his inwardness blooming outward. He stayed for a while, earned the right to leave in search of quietude and focus, and then, freed of the city, did something quietly monumental for the ages. "Choose to choose, choose to go," sang Lou Reed in 1967, a couple of years after York packed up for Southampton, leaving a Manhattan newly filled with Pop art. York is dead now, but you don't have to be dead to be gone, and just because you're gone doesn't mean you're not here; quite the opposite, sometimes. Ask Stanley Brouwn, if you see him. And say hi from me.

1. This is not to decry post-medium and cross-genre activity, merely to note that it can function as an expansion of public presence.
2. Alexander Koch has suggested that this type of dissent runs in cycles: he notes that artists demanded change particularly around 1870, 1917, 1968, and 1989, when seismic political changes were afoot, and certainly one can key a number of the practices in this book to those times. See Alexander Koch, *General Strike: KOW Issue 8* (Berlin: KOW, 2011).
3. If, as is the case, the majority of artists discussed here are American, then there are two reasons for that: the twentieth century was largely the American century in art; and America might be said to have perfected the excesses that would make an artist want to leave—the metropolitan crush, the hyper-capitalist art market, the hype machine.
4. Quoted in Calvin Tomkins, *Marcel Duchamp: The Afternoon Interviews* (Brooklyn, NY: Badlands Unlimited, 2013), 29.
5. Nor an essay on Lee Lozano, doyenne of withdrawal artists, about whom I have nothing much to add to what has been admirably written by others, particularly Sarah Lehrer-Graiwer and Bruce Hainley. Nor essays on figures such as Joseph Cornell or On Kawara, for similar reasons.
6. See Yves Klein, *The Foundations of Judo* (London: Everyday Press, 2009).
7. Alexander Koch, who organized the pioneering exhibition "Gestures of Disappearance" in 2002 at KOW, Berlin, and has regularly focused on artists who stop making art ever since, and Bob Nickas, who in his writing, curating, and teaching has focused particularly on women artists who've dropped out, have long done vital work in this direction.
8. A whole separate essay, of course, resides in the meaning of "necessary" here.

On and Off the Grid

I was standing among *The Islands*, twelve unearthly canvases in manifold grades of white and fairest blue that Agnes Martin painted in 1979, but I wasn't thinking about them. A couple of rooms earlier in Tate Modern I'd read the text Martin wrote concerning her 1973 sequence of screen prints, *On a Clear Day*: "These prints express innocence of mind. If you can go with them and hold your mind as empty and tranquil as they are and recognize your feelings at the same time you will realize your full response to this work." An invite with an afterglow, yet *The Islands*—quiet brimming things after the eye retunes, their sangfroid surprisingly welcoming, the horizontal lines dividing and pinning their paleness massy with auspicious imperfections—also reminded me of something. I felt it, thickly, in the hailing light.

In the early attainment stage of sitting Zen, zazen, thought evaporates through focus on the breath and the ensuing clarity is mobilized in various ways toward the remote goal of enlightenment. Without an empty mind there are things you can't feel, can't reach. In Martin's case, what's cached in her art for the disposed, quieted viewer—who has substituted febrile analysis with receiving—can be as simple and as complicated as happiness. Now, this meditative connection is perilous: subjective, and precisely the kind of interpretative link Martin issued injunctions against. But it's also as natural as breathing. Though Martin wasn't doctrinaire in anything except delivering her own opinions, she studied Zen Buddhism and Taoism, plus—to quote Jacquelynn Baas's summary—"Old Testament Calvinism, expressions of visionary Christianity, Platonism, transcendentalism [and] Vedanta."[1] D. T. Suzuki lectured in New York in the '50s and it's been posited that Martin went to hear him (her close friend Ad Reinhardt was beguiled by Far Eastern philosophical traditions), and an undated letter to her long-standing gallerist Arne Glimcher—in which she apostrophizes the Buddha's "Flower Sermon"—clarifies she worked on koans. Glimcher has also written that Martin "meditated daily."[2] This eastward lean was not, of course, wholly unusual in the keener corners of postwar America. But Glimcher adds, as Martin would have done, that there is "nothing mystical" about her work,[3] and equally vouchsafed that in *The Islands* and elsewhere is a hardheaded pragmatism of the plains that nevertheless veers toward the transcendent, a voiding unto serenity in readiness for "inspiration."

Martin, who at least outwardly didn't give a damn what the world thought, and who famously christened a 1997 sextet of paintings *With My Back to the World*, spoke recurrently about inspiration and the mental decor necessary to receive it: "empty," "untroubled." In 1972, four years after she relocated to the New Mexico desert where she would live for another forty-two years, she said: "I used to look in my mind for the unwritten page. If my mind was empty enough I could see it."[4] In Mary Lance's serene documentary *Agnes Martin: With My Back to the World*, completed in 2003, a year before the artist's death at age ninety-two, Martin says that "if your mind is full of garbage, if an inspiration came you wouldn't recognize it anyway. So you have to practice quiet, empty mind."

The consequence of her assiduous self-questing, no matter what traditions she drew on, is well known: decades of luminous, humming condensations of emotion in reductive pictorial form, works as democratically buoying, assuming you give them your time, as Bach or Mozart (Martin preferred Beethoven, though he unsettled her; she played Bach every day to remain "balanced").[5] To get there herself, though—and one of the many contradictions in her life and character is that she was essentially railroaded toward contentment—Martin had to perform a double withdrawal. Circumstances led her to turn her back on people, transferring from city to desert and, for the most part, living wholly alone. And she had to shift from the collective sphere of facts—illusory to her, founded on naught—into the annulled bays of her own head, so that emptiness might be returned, coherent and convivial, to others.

❀

"If you're alone you focus in on everything. You're just affected by everything. The sky and wind and air and nature, all of nature, and you're responding 100 percent. The best moments of my life

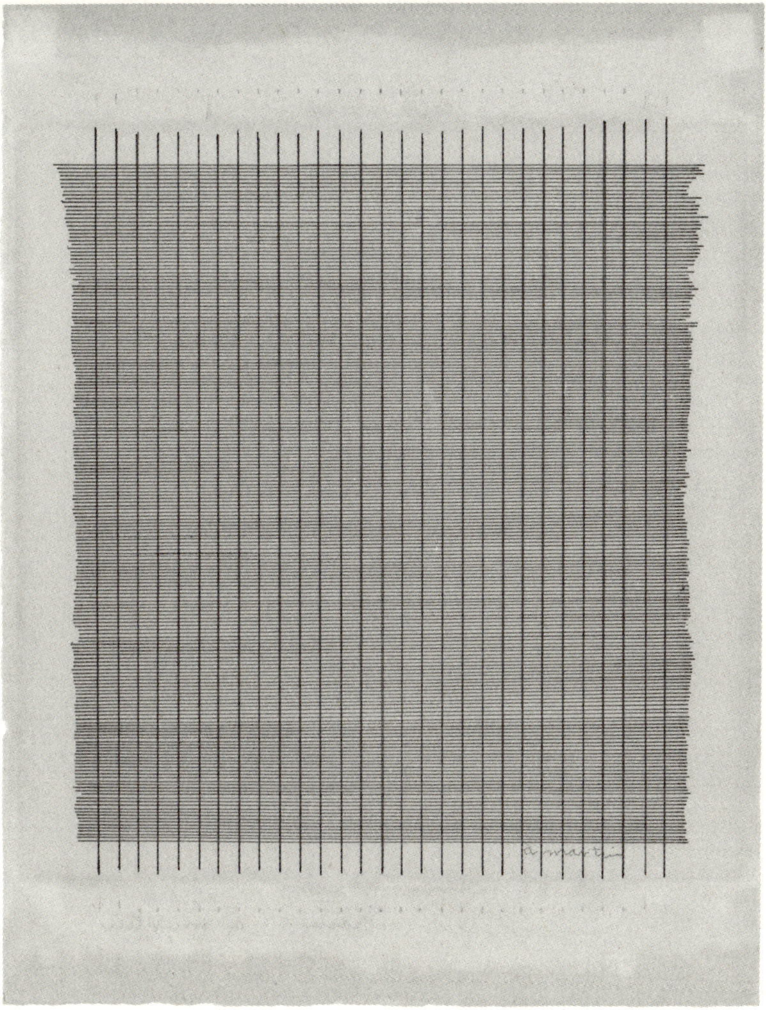

Agnes Martin, *Tremolo*, 1962

were when I was alone, the most enlightening and therefore the happiest," Martin says in Lance's documentary. However much she had explored solitude before—one might imagine it began involuntarily during her childhood when her mother would use silence as punishment—in 1967 her self-isolation began in earnest. In that year, at the age of fifty-five, she spent the money from a grant on a pickup truck and caravan and lit out from New York—the city she had arrived in fifteen years before at the urging of gallerist Betty Parsons, after living and working in New Mexico since the mid-1940s—traveling the United States for eighteen months.

By this time she had made the major breakthrough in her art: the discovery of the grid. But we can also discern a medley of reasons why she might abandon the city, wrapping her troubles in distance. In 1962 Martin had been hospitalized in Bellevue for schizophrenia, receiving electroshock treatment before her friends could stop it, after being discovered wandering catatonic in Manhattan. Shock had not cured her. She heard voices, dropped into trances, and clung to omens, and particularly for such a person certain other events perhaps served as beckoning off-ramps. Martin had recently lost to developers her paradisiacal (to a cognoscente of austerity) studio in a heatless one-hundred-foot-long sailmaker's loft on Coenties Slip, Lower Manhattan, where for years she had painted and lived a disciplined life alongside Ellsworth Kelly, Robert Indiana, and James Rosenquist, with Jasper Johns and Robert Rauschenberg for neighbors. The same day she was told the building would be torn down, she received a grant, the means to buy a vehicle and leave. Reinhardt had just died of a heart attack at the age of fifty-three. Martin's relationship with Greek artist Chryssa, whom Glimcher remembers as "much more violently psychotic than Agnes,"[6] had apparently just ended; after this she would have no others. (In the documentary she says, again echoing Buddhist thought, that she had lived many lives before in which she was married and had children, and this time had asked to live alone.)

She was, furthermore, apparently experiencing a self-lacerating relationship to pride resulting from the amplified attention her art was now receiving. (When her new home in the desert was taken from her a few years later, she said she'd deserved it, that she'd been too prideful again.) Relatedly, she had been embraced

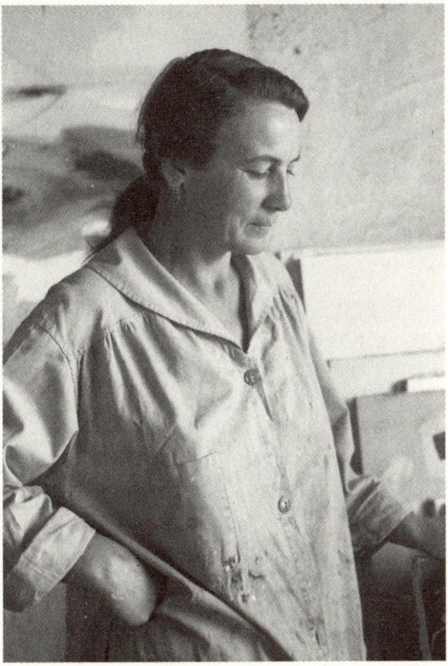

Agnes Martin in her studio in New Mexico, 1953

by the Minimalist contingent of artists, exhibiting alongside whom she would later claim—as a self-declared Abstract Expressionist, an artist of feelings—to have been "a mistake." We don't know the ranking of these dynamics. Martin, as Nancy Princenthal recounts in her 2015 biography of the artist, said various things. In 1981 she said, "I came to a place of recognition of confusion that had to be solved. [...] I waited patiently for [...] something like permission to leave," which she goes on to say came after a show in Los Angeles. In 1983, she said: "I left New York in 1967 because every day I suddenly felt I wanted to die and it was connected with painting. It took me several years to find out that the cause was an overdeveloped sense of responsibility." In 1996 she said that it was connected with the loss of her loft. At another point, Princenthal recounts, Martin said she recognized she had already made some "masterful" paintings and so she could leave.[7] The story kept changing, or all the aspects mattered to changing degrees.

She went, and in 1968 a vision of an adobe hut fetched her back to New Mexico, where, renting a patch of land on a faraway mesa in Sandoval County (her voices apparently told her not to buy, just as they later said she couldn't have a garden), she erected an adobe and log house and, in 1972, a studio, and managed without television, radio, newspapers, telephone, or electricity. She collected rainwater to drink. When she began making art again it was because she was approached with a proposal to make a set of prints, and because, her reputation apparently swelling further in her absence, a curator at the Institute of Contemporary Art in Philadelphia invited her to have a retrospective. The print series, made in Germany, turned out to be the thirty-part *On a Clear Day*: a deeply satisfying mathematical group of grids, among her last—closing of the old road, commencement of the new.

Martin's remembrance of how she originally discovered the grid doesn't quite fit the evidence. She spoke of a grid rising in her mind as she ruminated on innocence, the upshot being *The Tree* (1964), though she had in fact been painting grids since around 1960. One change in the interim—what might mark the later grids as different, new—was their diffusion to the canvas edge, delivering objecthood to the painting. The grid Martin described in 1967 was a lightening, a de-monumentalizing: "When I cover the square surface with rectangles, it lightens the weight of the square, destroys its power."[8] This airborne quality is key. "In the eye [the grid] jiggles loose and hovers," Peter Schjeldahl has written, persuasively. "Edge and shape, figure and ground, and matter and atmosphere are reversible, bringing about, for me, a sense of oscillation in the optic nerve."[9] That reversibility might also be associated with interdependence and mutual support, the oscillation delivering a kind of blissfulness of balance. Certainly degrees of delight are the terms in which Martin couched her work. She spoke, in 1981, of shifting, albeit within the diapason of suddenly experienced and fugitive emotions, from joy to happiness, in the spell between the last works made in New York and *On a Clear Day*.[10]

The year after producing these prints, inspired anew by them, Martin broke a nearly eight-year spell of not painting. When she did—offering the completed paintings to Glimcher's gallery, Pace, who gladly took them—she unbuckled the grid, abbreviating it to the horizontal stripe, a format again open to interpretation. Not that interpretation is the point. (Experience is.) Martin now also began using color more readily, if parsimoniously: pastel pinks and blues and yellows, watery oxidized reds and ochers. One might (many have) hallucinate in them New Mexico landscapes—peachy glare as native light, adobe ciphered in dusty reds—and be led astray. A local world glimmers in the work but, when indulged, it weighs the paintings down, limits them. Martin spoke about her feel for the flat landscape, the impression of expanding over the plane, but also of her paintings' horizontals in no way *representing* that; rather, she suggested, the viewer moves inward over the line. This gravitational drag is the signature course of Martin's art. The mind, not receiving quick distraction, slows, the eye pasturing appreciatively, tiny shifts starting to count—barely perceptible color voicings, eccentricities of pencil and paint application—the whole commencing to hum, to pull. If there is gentle blaze to the work then it isn't keyed to something in the world. It feels grander yet more internalized than that, and as such strongly associable with the abstract values Martin would talk about, happiness or subsets of happiness like amity. Facing the canvas, her language becomes plausible, even if we wonder how much we were primed.

One might also think, at some point—it's inevitable if you know the biography—of what's bridled by those horizontal lines and convivial colors on those consistently square canvases. Throughout her life, though she took medication after a certain point, Martin continued to endure schizophrenic episodes, evidently deciding to face these alone. That aforementioned abortive relationship, whose ending can't be fully factored out of her self-isolation, and her sexuality per se, constitute a black box that those close to Martin refuse to speculate on. One might think, too, of her upbringing with an extremely disciplinarian Presbyterian mother, which Martin claimed to value while also telling writers she had suffered emotional abuse. Leonard Cohen once remarked concerning his own time in a Zen monastery that nobody goes to such a place who isn't already broken. It would be easy to look at the circumstances of Martin's life and call her damaged in several different ways, survey her consummate achievement, and footnote Edmund Wilson's 1941 essay collection on childhood psychological distress and artistry, "The Wound and the Bow." Martin wasn't a transcendent individual: she was patched together as we all are. She was an ascetic who liked fast cars, her art drew on the landscape but didn't, she officially discovered the grid four years after she really did, and so on.

But the art—which in any case she didn't even attempt when suffering visitations, waiting them out—shimmers on the other side of all this. A beaming white matrix of fine vertical rectangles like *Morning* (1965) is cool Euclidean precision commuted by light and dimensional definitude, made approachable—humanized—by Martin's faintly quavering fist. Later work such as *Happy Holiday* (1999), banded alternations of tempered apricot and light blue, gives one a flash of brickwork and empyrean in midday whiteout before dispensing with such associations and asserting zest distilled, a portable sweet spot. At such moments, Martin makes you forget all about her and about everything else, but you have to wait for that to happen, become like a pond without ripples; her embarkation becomes yours but thinking won't help you go there. "Dependence on the intellect," Martin wrote in a notebook, "is so thoroughly taught that some people think they would die if they stopped thinking."[11] It is this insistence on being egalitarian and outsmarting the brain-smart that makes Martin at once hugely accessible and, in the postwar settlement of art as a custom of intellection, a wordless challenge.

In 2004 the artist who lived on rainwater and drove a white BMW, who painted abstract works all her life and then closed with a petite sketch of a pot plant, went into the light, leaving her accumulated light behind. The following spring, under a full moon in the garden of the Harwood Museum of Art in Taos—clandestinely, against New Mexico law, despite her own work being in their collection—her ashes were placed in a Japanese bowl lined with gold leaf, then scattered in dug-out ground among the roots of an apricot tree. Out in the world, Facebook had recently launched and YouTube was about to go live; the world, plunging into accelerated connection and distraction and superficies, turning its back ever more emphatically upon Martin's self-designed model of soulful quiescence. "In my best moments," she once wrote, "I think 'life has passed me by,' and I am content."[12] Glimcher sang favorite songs to her in her last days and sometimes she sang along. "She liked *Blue Skies*," he would later write.[13] Martin's final painting comprises two wide bands of white dividing a sallow squall of gray. Rain will fall but tranquillity is always there, behind the clouds. And there's no rain, and there are no clouds.

1. Jacquelynn Baas, "Agnes Martin: Readings for Writings," in *Agnes Martin*, ed. Frances Morris and Tiffany Bell (London: Tate Publishing, 2015), 224.
2. Arne Glimcher, *Agnes Martin: Paintings, Writings, Remembrances* (London: Phaidon Press, 2012), 10.
3. Ibid.
4. Agnes Martin, "The Untroubled Mind," in ibid., 218.
5. See Nancy Princenthal, *Agnes Martin: Her Life and Art* (New York: Thames & Hudson, 2015), 237.
6. Glimcher, *Paintings, Writings, Remembrances*, 8.
7. Martin, cited in Princenthal, *Her Life and Art*, 147–48.
8. Martin, quoted in Lucy Lippard, "Homage to the Square," *Art in America* 4 (July–August 1967): 55.
9. Peter Schjeldahl, "Life Worker," *New Yorker*, June 7, 2004, http://www.newyorker.com/magazine/2004/06/07/life-work-2.
10. See Morris and Bell, *Agnes Martin*, 29n33.
11. Notebook page, reproduced in Glimcher, *Paintings, Writings, Remembrances*, 16.
12. Ibid., 201.
13. Ibid., 6.

The Next Hill

In 1963, in his thirty-fifth year, Albert York painted *Summer Trees*, a modestly scaled—30 × 34 cm—canvas that depicts a trio of trees clustered in a field. Their branches merge; indeed, everything here liquesces into everything else. The massed leaves, an intricacy of quick green dabs, disperse tints of themselves into gunmetal air, trunks sink into grassland the color of their foliage. This isn't a painting of discrete elements but a unity, earth-sky-trees-light. It's a holism that also, when considered closely, treats time in surprising ways, suggesting both past—looking, remembering, restructuring, converting—and future, for within the painting some rural revelation is afoot. Soft whiteness breaks on the horizon though the hour is ambiguous, and the trees are not centered but pushed to one side, leaving a pregnant gap leftward. Perhaps whatever abstract force is surging forth will fill it, or so you're invited to think by the weird certitude, the apparent heart song, of *Summer Trees*. That force might be confederacy with the real—"I believe we live in a paradise, I really do," is one of a handful of quotes we have from York[1]—or, more reflexively, the autonomous life of a painting whose subject is, in part, the trepidations of seeing itself.

Summer Trees was among the nineteen then new paintings in York's first one-person show at New York's Davis Galleries, now Davis & Langdale, from March to April 1963. The summer of those trees was likely that of '62, the year he left the city and moved to East Hampton, Long Island, with his wife and two stepchildren. In 1963, after most of the paintings in that debut exhibition (which garnered positive reviews) sold, York quit commuting to his Manhattan framing job—his own paintings are not neatly framed but, when framed at all, often sport roughshod rims with smudgy crimson borders that set off his greens—opting instead for house painting and local carpentry work that gave him ready access to the panel scraps he preferred working on. He made more paintings to augment his earnings. He delivered them to Roy Davis at first by hand, in a brown paper bag, and then—in an emphatic break with the city and the mechanisms of its art world—by mail, wrapped in brown paper.

We're entering this story at midpoint, though. York's parents separated when he was young—he grew up believing his mother was dead—and following a childhood and adolescence spent bouncing between Michigan and Ontario (where he studied art in Toronto), he was drafted, serving in Korea in the early 1950s. Demobbed, he took evening painting classes at the Art Students League of New York, worked dead-end jobs that left him too tired to paint, and become a gilder at Kulicke Frames, a Manhattan framer. One task there, framing hundreds of paintings by Giorgio Morandi for the artist's first US retrospective in 1957, gave York renewed confidence and he began painting again in 1959/60. In summer 1960, at the urging of his future wife, Virginia, whom he had met the year before, the couple spent four months in France—Paris, Sens, Toulon, Marseilles—where York painted small, dark canvases in plein air. ("Murk and gloom," says York expert William Corbett of the one he saw.)[2] On returning, he took up his framing job once more, began going to work at 5 a.m. to have time to paint in daylight (again outdoors, in Central Park, on small, oddly dimensioned, non-geometric wood panels), and started prowling the Metropolitan Museum of Art. He learned from Cézanne, Manet, the Ashcan School, and—most of all, he would tell the *New Yorker*'s Calvin Tomkins—Albert Pinkham Ryder, with his compositional smarts and compact scales. (In this, his one major interview, York never mentions contemporaries working figuratively in the wake of Abstract Expressionism, like Milton Avery or Fairfield Porter, a lacuna that has left critic and York aficionado Bruce Hainley suspicious.)[3]

A coworker at the framers', Jerry Anderson, saw his paintings and suggested he show them to the business's owner, an artist. The latter in turn mentioned them to Roy Davis, who had run his own gallery for a decade. Of the first show that Davis gave York, Lawrence Campbell remarked in a 1963 *Art News* review: "Albert York is a new discovery. He has blushed unseen in East Hampton for some time."[4] York would blush more, be seen less. Clearly there was a temperamental explanation, extreme personal reticence: York's colleagues at the framers' remembered him as extraordinarily shy and monosyllabic, and a doubtful legend subsists—supposedly Virginia said to Davis that she didn't know he painted until six weeks after they were married.

But look at the canvases, which Campbell rightly noted as being by a "specialist in very tiny, important differences"—distinctions that demand slow, watchful, sensitized looking and exacting staging. Look at *Twin Trees* (ca. 1963), a burnished-gold dreamscape set again at a mysterious hour—it's reduced to a couple of shades, and moonlight or pre-storm weather will do that but not *these* darkly regal tones—and merging realistic landscape description with the mystic charge of Samuel Palmer and the reductive heat of certain Pinkham Ryders. The trees here are entities, animist creatures; the pool reflecting one of them is an entity too. Barely perceptible touches of rogue color come to complicate: the horizon's reddish tint, jade smears at the pool's edge. They function like clues to how the little canvas tugs so hard. The aforementioned Porter, writing about this work in 1975, notes that York's paintings "contain an emotion that he has discovered outside himself," and that *Two Trees* "is for [York] the source of his imagination of the trees' lifelong experience. These two trees could be Baucis and Philemon after Zeus, at their death, changed them into trees to grant them their desire never to be separated."[5] The rhetorical flight is indicative in itself.

Connecting York's lifestyle choices to his remarkable art, one might extrapolate that to paint like this—imbricating massiveness in the minor, not recording but building, poiesis—meant being out there, out of town, slowed in green air at a moment when the improvisatory torrents of Abstract Expressionism, which York didn't care for, had ceded to Pop. Simultaneous with his Davis show was the Guggenheim Museum's Lawrence Alloway-curated "Six Painters and the Object," featuring Robert Rauschenberg, Jim Dine, Jasper Johns, Roy Lichtenstein, James Rosenquist, and Andy Warhol, a development York didn't care for either. Nothing could be more alien to his slowly accreting, tremulous attentiveness than a silk screen of an industrial product, painting as mechanical swiping; no city was more Pop than the one he was leaving. (One can of course speculate to what degree York's antithetical approach to prevailing currents helped sell his work to buyers, including Jacqueline Onassis and Lauren Bacall, just as one can wonder to what extent his distanced outlook was

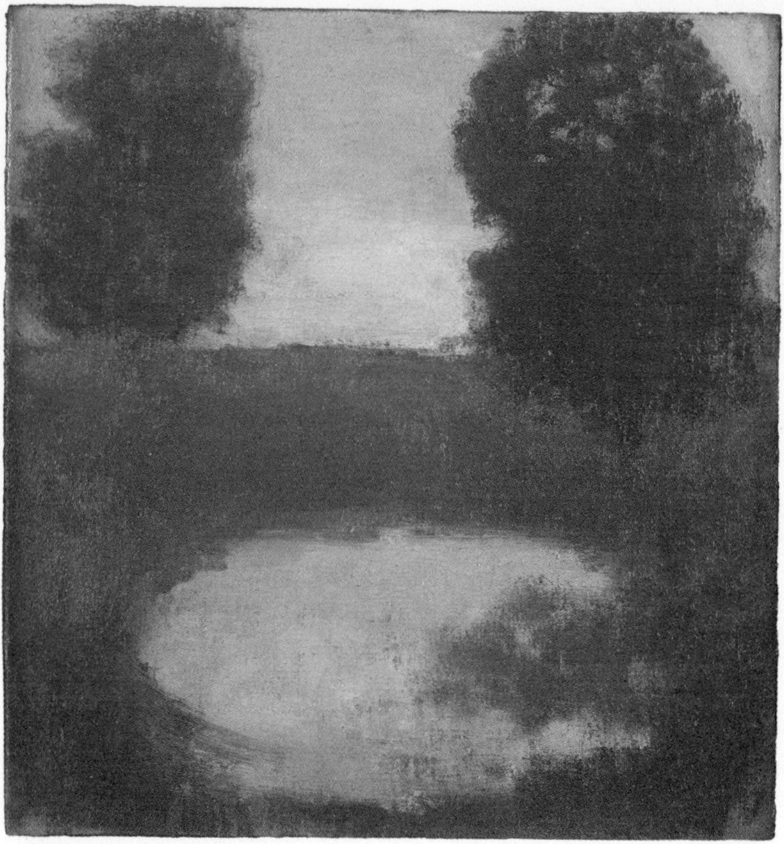

Albert York, *Twin Trees*, ca. 1963

annealed by a childhood of estrangement from his own family—no mother to speak of, time spent farmed out to relatives and boarding school.)

This breakaway of York's was, however, only the first of several, each a circumstantial permission to burrow deeper. As the 1960s went on, his painting divided into landscapes, still lifes—zinnias with the hard-won architectonic weight of Morandi's stolid vessels—and increasingly estranged outdoor figures. See the airborne, centaur-ish *Flying Figure in Landscape* (1967), whose unreality irradiates York's calmer landscapes, similar to how Stanley Spencer's 1930s studies of English allotments are ghosted with that eccentric religiosity he essayed elsewhere. York's rural views intermittently transmute, turn tropical, and snakes repeatedly appear, obvious symbols modified by a context of muteness. In 1972 his father, dying of cancer, told York his mother was in fact alive and working as a real-estate broker in Florida and, following the death of the man she'd later married, wanted to see him. They met; it was, the artist would report, "pretty rough." York's father died in 1973. "Some years later," writes Tomkins, "York began receiving a small income from a trust fund that his mother had set up in his name. The Davises say that it was harder to get pictures out of him after that."[6]

This intractability can't be divorced from his art, which over a decade or so from the late '60s onward enacts a steady rotation inward, while its iconography expands, growing shaggy at the edges. Increasingly, the real world and the psychological world interpenetrate. York continued to paint self-described "potboiler" pictures of cows—heavy with flesh and chambered portent—but other charged elements enter the mix. Animals tend to register here as blank yet silently intelligent—see the giant feline in York's idiosyncratic recast of Manet's *Olympia* (1863), *Reclining Female Nude with Cat* (1978), or the tensile dogs in *Brown Dog and Grey Dog in Landscape* (1978), both fixated on something out of frame. Indians—"not 'Native Americans' but belong[ing] to another time," Corbett writes[7]—appear on horseback or paired, held wide apart in the frame, as in *Landscape with Two Indians* (1978), a sluggish snake before them. The snake appears repeatedly in York's paintings, low and centered, not acting, not benign. Waiting.

Or tropical palms float back like dreams. Or nudes and skeletons and, reflecting York's time in Florida, crocodiles flicker. Or flowers in pots and glass goblets—arranged for what? Hainley pertinently asks—come to feel absolutely enormous. This is the vortex of York's work: *something* is forever transpiring, the visible has a barn-heavy weight—in a heifer's dark orbs, the solid air between two figures, what a dog senses and leans its body toward—but the viewer isn't privy. What York builds, despite being a deeply figurative painter, is closer to an abstraction, a scattered archipelago whose glowing islands one wants to bridge. Decades before the vexed speculations of the object-oriented ontology school of philosophy, he posits objects—which includes animals—as having inner selves that are impenetrable yet spark out aspects of what Graham Harman calls eidos: that which belongs to the shuttered real within. The sparks themselves, all that make it onto canvas, dazzle.

❀

Yet this is not a transcendental story but a workmanlike brawl, the sparks coming from daily hammering, the results conveying modernist overtones of a knot-brained tussle with the motif. It begins with the necessary retreat in order for the struggle to take place—space cleared for a fight. "Some development of the capacity to be alone," writes Anthony Storr in his book *Solitude*, "is necessary if the brain is to function at its best, and if the individual is to fulfil his highest potential. Human beings easily become alienated from their own deepest needs and feelings. Learning, thinking, innovation, and maintaining contact with one's own inner world are all facilitated by solitude."[8] In York's case, this must have hurt. The remove required to establish his clandestine network was also, it appears, time and space enough to breed deep inward dissatisfaction. "What Al doesn't understand is that in art you never quite hit what you're aiming at, but the difference may not be downward," Tomkins quotes York's former employer Robert Kulicke as saying.[9] York did not destroy his own art, à la Frenhofer, the solitary painter—with whom Cézanne famously identified—in Balzac's "The Unknown Masterpiece" (1831). But he resisted an institutional retrospective for a long time and when his work went out into the world and he saw it, the effects were deleterious.

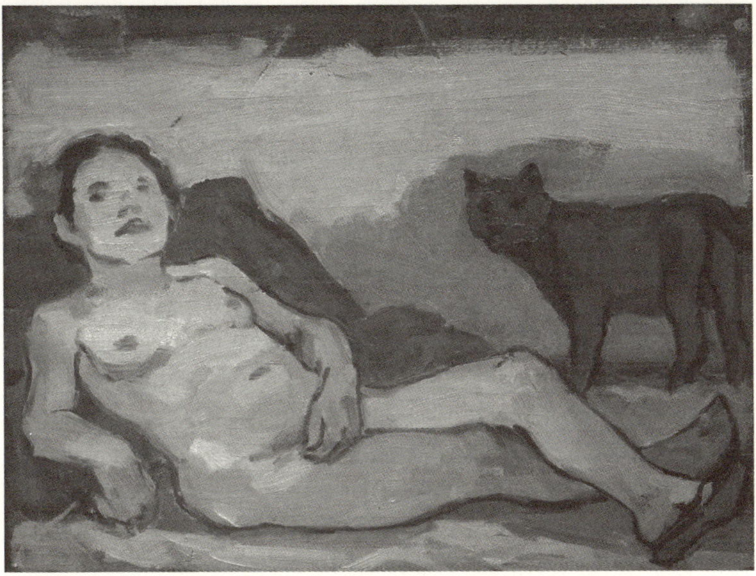

Albert York, *Reclining Female Nude with Cat*, 1978

Prior to this, the further outward he could go, the better. Between 1982 and '83, he and his wife lived apart and York painted some fifteen paintings while living, with a dog, in rented properties in Long Island: a particularly productive year, one of dark blooms. Among the outcrops was *Two Pink Anemones in a Glass Vase in a Landscape* (1982). The stolidity of the motif, while beautiful, repels. There's a surreal disjuncture astir—the still life is outside—which ought to feel minor but, in its conflating of specific genres, feels large, not least because the foregrounded subject has the monumental wrongness of one of Magritte's apples colonizing a room, seeming to objectify the heresy. The simple floral arrangement in a fat low glass is embedded, immovable, yet it sits there like a heavy-shadowed abstract problem, each flower weighing a ton. The painting suggests that one might take any object and stare at it until, like a word regarded too long, it abstracts—it threatens as the factness of objects threatens and disgusts the subject of Jean-Paul Sartre's *Nausea* (1938). Just two flowers, but you'll never, ever know them. You can only relay the attempt, the rebuff; the passing beauty of the trying, as Blake had it, "To see a world in a grain of sand, / And a heaven in a wild flower, / Hold infinity in the palm of your hand, / And eternity in an hour."[10]

York seems more pragmatist than mystic. Nerve is needed to return to this complex of observational difficulty, to chip away at it, and if working in seclusion from an art world by now caught up in Neo-Expressionism—the Schnabels and Salles of this world—spurred him to do so, engaging with his work's public life was reciprocally risky. A major museum display of York's work opened at the Boston Museum of Fine Arts in 1982, a show also featuring Alex Katz, Willem de Kooning, Jane Freilicher, and Richard Diebenkorn, all represented by single paintings. York had twenty-one works on show. It's not known if he saw that exhibition. In 1989, though, the curator Klaus Kertess put York's work in a show with April Gornik and again with Freilicher. York, kept out of the negotiations, did see the show toward the end of its run and "came away in despair," says Corbett.[11] "It's pretty lousy—pardon the word—work," he told Tomkins.[12] Three years later he sent his last painting to Davis & Langdale, having made, it is estimated, some three hundred paintings in his lifetime. (He continued for some time to draw.)

Maybe, for him, the notion of public viewing rendered the work unacceptably vulnerable: all those eyes discerning potential flaws, missing the achievements. Maybe, conversely, praise felt like misreading. Or perhaps, like artists and writers and musicians who turn their back on what they've done once they've done it so as to move on, York simply worked in a slash-and-burn manner, finishing a canvas and sending it away to wipe the slate clean and improve with the next. Whatever: we have the work and he had his discontent with what, of his seeing, he managed to limn. The Japanese artist Hiroshi Sugimoto once told me that an effect of the seascape photographs he made was a "powering-up of the eye": the more you look the more you can see. Consider such a process in York's case, or speculate on the same with the results before you. One might think that all he did was look, render, frown, try again while the world thickened around him; sight outpacing facility, as he saw it, as he felt it.

When the double bind is this patent—finesse perception so far and with what others regard as such terrific results and common air becomes intolerable—the romance of withdrawal curdles quickly. The loner becomes even more alone, in a shell within a shell. Nobody's counsel counts but one's own, particularly when the effort is to translate what nobody else has experienced, a private spectrum of being that, the results suggest, stretches from unease to paradisiacal transport to both at once. As such, the notion that York's *other* apparent subject in his art is the fact that, yes, this *is* just paint, may not be modernist thinking—though it chimes with it—but a frustration with the intransigence of his medium. His pas de deux with materiality could be read as a wish for wizard fingers, the stuff to do his bidding, an apologia in advance, as well as a model of figurative painting as the existentialist absurd incarnate. Satisfaction whistles perpetually from behind the next hill, behind the next unpainted uneven slat. At the time, and decades later, an audience—lured by the triple appeal of the slow nature they hardly ever see, the dream of departure, sheer vicariousness—cheers him on, unheard.

1. Albert York, cited in Calvin Tomkins, "Profile: Artist Unknown," *New Yorker*, June 19, 1994, 76.
2. William Corbett, *Albert York* (Brooklyn, NY: Pressed Wafer Books, 2010), 11.
3. See Bruce Hainley, "Pitch Notes for Albert York," in *Albert York* (New York: Matthew Marks Gallery; Davis & Langdale Company, 2014), 128.
4. Lawrence Campbell, *Art News* review (1963), in ibid., 159, fig. 6.
5. Fairfield Porter, "Albert York" (1975), in ibid., 23.
6. Tomkins, "Artist Unknown," 74.
7. Corbett, in *Albert York* (2010), 19.
8. Anthony Storr, *Solitude: A Return to the Self* (New York: Free Press, 2005), 28.
9. Robert Kulicke, cited in Tomkins, "Artist Unknown," 81.
10. William Blake, "Augeries of Innocence," lines 1–4.
11. Corbett, in *Albert York* (2010), 23.
12. Tomkins, "Artist Unknown," 81.

Manufacturing Dissent

It's a Saturday afternoon in 2013, the Year of the Snake, and I'm standing in the low-slung postindustrial Berlin showrooms of a German art collector who, yearly, displays a thematic edit of her collection. This time she has consulted the Chinese zodiac: we're invited, amid a knowing conflation of the curatorial and the dictatorial, to see serpentine lines everywhere, whatever the artist's original intentions. Bordered by a Joachim Koester video, a Franz West seat, and a spiraling Richard Deacon sculpture, one of Charlotte Posenenske's "Vierkantrohre" series or "Square Tubes Series"—linear assemblies of hollow, four-sided, galvanized steel tubes and angled connectors, resembling ventilation pipes—rises up python-like. The intervention, as the collector's smile affirms, is high-toned, dumb-smart. Of all the artists numbered here, Posenenske most decidedly sanctioned her art's reformatting in whatever shape or form the buyer desired. This zoomorphic rendering, complicatedly dated 1967–2009 and also 2013, for its conceptual inception, fabrication, and current configuration, may be cartoonish but it doesn't violate the magnanimous modular spirit of the late German artist's work. Rather, the specific form and private-collection context open up questions originally encoded into it, making them irrepressible.

Posenenske had been gone twenty-four years by the time this work was manufactured—her estate, administered by her second husband, Burkhard Brunn, sanctions the nonprofit sale of unlimited new versions of these works at cost—and prior to her death in October 1985 it had been over fifteen years since she cared about the art world, or at least participated in it. Famously, she began a full disengagement from contemporary art amid the ructions of 1968. At age thirty-seven, she stopped exhibiting and accepting commissions, dispatched her remaining artworks to an attic, and embarked on a degree in sociology. Focusing on factory work and assessments of its value, she devoted the rest of her life to, as Brunn puts it, "breaking asunder the rigid standardization of factory labor in favor of extended codetermination."[1] While she studied, she and her husband wrote guiding sentences in pencil on the white headboard of their bed, including one by Goethe that translates, approximately, as: "And time and time again they raised theory to the level of practice." The snake in the Sammlung Hoffmann was, and is, theory.

Posenenske's theorizing, which resulted in some three hundred artworks between 1956–68—though her practice only really took off three years before she quit—was formed in what might from a distance look like a crucible of deep idealism, one that followed a harrowing childhood in Nazi Germany. In 1940, when she was nine, her father, who was Jewish (her mother was not) poisoned himself, convinced he would imminently be sent to a concentration camp. Posenenske saw the body and the shock led her to abandon the outside world and cocoon herself; she became an obsessive reader, a reader of absolutely anything. Two years later she was told that being half-Jewish she had to leave school: she "escaped deportation herself only because a sympathetic local police officer hid her file."[2] Reinstated in education after the war's end, she went on to study in Stuttgart with the artist Willi Baumeister, who introduced her, as Brunn has elsewhere written, "to the socially related notions of order of Neo-Plasticism (Mondrian), to the socio-revolutionary principles of creation in Soviet constructivism (El Lissitzky), and to the uncompromising ideas of progress, standardization, collective work and anonymity."[3] These social groundings for art making would be decisive.

While a student in the early 1950s, Posenenske adopted a classically stern, minimal-modernist aesthetic: stark white walls, long travels to obtain the perfect plug socket, admiring readings of Adolf Loos's *Ornament and Crime* (1908). At a certain point, though, she quit her studies and for unaccountable reasons—a tricky affair with Baumeister has been mooted (a photo exists of Posenenske posing nude for him)—relocated to the city of Lübeck and joined a theater group, working as a stage designer from 1952 to 1955. (Again, here one might feel the components of her later work, with its farsighted, proto-relational participatory aspect and neo-Constructivist industrial aesthetic, snapping together.) When she renewed her art practice in the mid-1950s, Posenenske again accentuated the industrial, the impersonal: her "Rasterbilder"

(Raster images) paintings of 1956–57, graphic patterns of circles and semicircles, suggest primitive electronic imagery; her "Spachtelarbeiten" (Palette-knife works), and "Spritzbilder" (Sprayed pictures) (both 1964), none publicly exhibited in her lifetime, furthered an impersonal mode of abstraction divorced from the hand and rooted in the prewar European modernism she had studied. From here, Posenenske unwaveringly worked away from flatness, first toward the self-exposing illusionistic depth of her "Plastiches Bilder" (Sculptural pictures, 1965–66)—assured conversations between folded surfaces and advancing and receding colors—and later the more explicitly objectified 1967 "Reliefs" series, wherein she transitioned, too, to the amendable form. (After this, color fades out, natural light henceforth employed as a collaborator, providing differently shadowed and illuminated aspects of white and gray surfaces.)

All of which would only count for so much had Posenenske not, as she went, also rigorously dissolved her own authority. By 1967 when she dreamed up the "Square Tubes Series" and began having them fabricated in steel and corrugated pasteboard, her conception of authorship and ownership had expanded and sophisticated radically. Equal in "producing" the sculptures, her "coauthors" included collectors, promoters, steel workers, transporters, installers, and "spiritual and financial supporters." The work, as she saw it, was akin to factory goods—she labeled her audience "consumers"—and was expressly a collective achievement. Collectivity extended to the owners refashioning the work's parts however they liked, and to Posenenske exhibiting outside of the gallery system—which she already had issues with—on a traffic island in Offenbach, for example. (Her sculptures, needless to say, were unsigned.) "The elements are reproducible, and the circulation is unlimited," she wrote, in 1968: "The parts are similar to prefabricated assembly parts, but are distinct from these in that they lack a use value and make a claim to be art. Aside from this claim, everything else about them is controllable."[4]

One might, as others have, see the "Square Tubes Series" as superbly drafted concords between the art world and the factory floor, undercutting the exclusivity and privilege of the one with a sharp blast of reality—and egoless communality—from the other. But Posenenske, who had seen the horrific side of systematic industrialization via the Nazi regime, departs from the chimerical tenets of Constructivism in decisive ways, and it's notable that in their echoes of and retreats from industrial conditions, the "Square Tubes Series" foreshadow the real-world quandaries of industrial standardization that she would spend her "second" career working to ameliorate. They are standardized objects designed to behave in non-standardized ways: they restore power to owners, they're intended to be unruly and subjectively slanted, they remain in flow. They reacted to the art market's profiteering preference for the unique, the one-off, but also to a narrow conformist ideology telescoped into labor practice.

Yet they fell short in one important way. Although they redistributed authorship, the "Square Tubes Series" did not allow audience interaction within the exhibition space. The nearest Posenenske came to this was in a 1967 group show—put together by future dealer Paul Maenz and artist Peter Roehr, lasting two hours and ten minutes, featuring art that couldn't be taken away, and entitled "All This, Sweetie, Will One Day Be Yours"—at Galerie Dorothea Loehr, a former farm building on the outskirts of Frankurt. Here, as archival photographs demonstrate, four men wearing Lufthansa overalls repeatedly reconfigured the artist's cumbrous cardboard-tube structures, responding to factors including the weather and the number of viewers. That, in the compelling post facto logic of Posenenske's progress, is why the "Drehflügel" (Turning leaves, or Turning wings) works were necessary, why they constitute a pellucid endpoint. In these 1967–68 object/environments, hinged panels can be opened or closed by viewers. Even as she made them, however, Posenenske was already just about done. "It is painful for me to face the fact that art cannot contribute to the solution of urgent social problems," she wrote, in Offenbach, in a statement on her work for the Swiss journal *Art International*, published in May 1968.[5] Sometime later she refused an invitation to propose a public art project in West Germany, writing that she resented how art was now an "alibi" used to soft-pedal "the slums of the future."[6]

The Occam's razor reading of this is that Posenenske had swung art as close to reality as possible and found it lacking, and had also been overtaken by events. In a year of rambunctious political activism she was asking her audience to enter a gallery and daintily revolve some metal sheets, as if doing so would

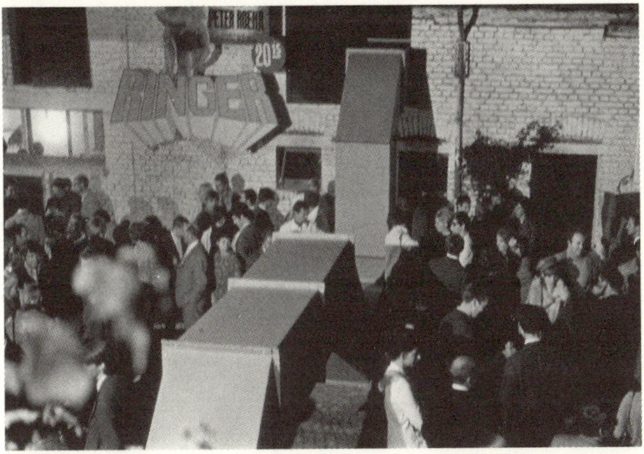

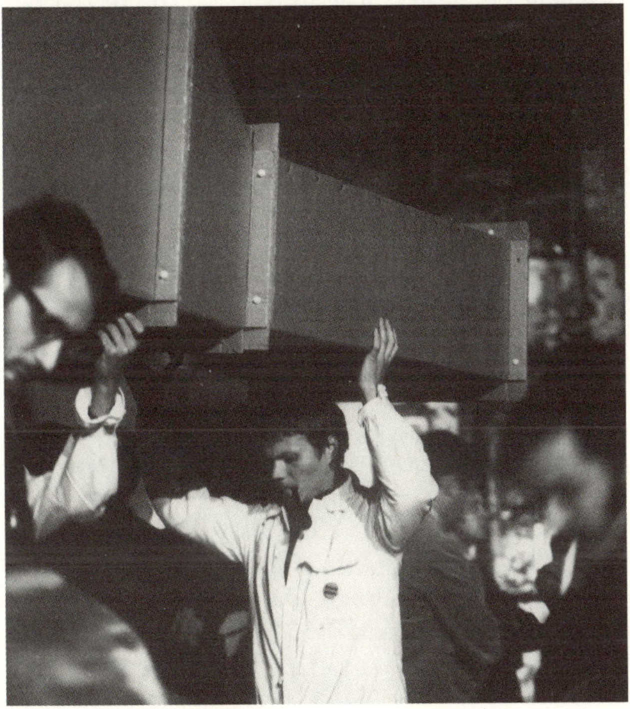

Handlers rearranging Charlotte Posenenske's
Square Tubes Series DW, Galerie Dorothea Loehr,
Frankfurt am Main, September 9, 1967

transform society in a trickle-down way while streets burned. While it pressured the context, this manifestly wasn't enough. A more affirming interpretation—that of art historian Christine Mehring, for example, who says that Posenenske, despite espousing hopeful aspects of her era's new interconnectedness, "was never an idealist"[7]—is that her works were a thrown towel, *designed* to illuminate the limits of art's agency, and that hands-on sociological work was not a disavowal of her previous position but absolutely continuous with it. (First, perform the limits of art vis-à-vis social change; second, do something that really contributes to it.) This, arguably, is to overlook the word "painful" in her 1968 statement,[8] and the fact that industrial sociology, as an alternative, is not directly "political" but academic.

More tenable might be a reading wherein Posenenske was lengthily trying, through her actions, to get somewhere and was honest enough to say when she hit an unassailable wall—a journeying and an ethical steadfastness that ought to be considered courageous enough in itself. Some artists seek and others find, Picasso noted; it seems obvious which Posenenske was, and the search went on inside and outside art. The latter, and sociological studies, might be construed as the accommodating acts of someone negotiating lifelong between working- and middle-class roots, between a learned love of idealistic art and its apparent underperformance in the real world (and in an art world that preaches to a miscellany of the converted and the disengaged), between political consciousness and what she could best do to live up to it.

Maybe her irresolution never stopped. Note this, as virtually none of her commentators do: "Shortly before she died," Brunn writes, "Charlotte Posenenske returned to art."[9] She stored the artworks that she "still accepted" in one room of her house, tossing out all the others—Brunn says he smashed them with a hammer. When Maenz asked to show her work, she was "very pleased and agreed to show her works which had not been presented for 20 years." Maybe she did want to come back, and maybe backsliding is not so terrible, illustrative as it might be of an art industry whose witch's brew of virtue and vice it is endlessly hard to be conclusive about. What kind of virtue is silence if your stand is forgotten by art history, as—at that time for Posenenske—it seemingly had been?

These questions remain forever tabled because the only person who could say for sure isn't around to answer them, and it's difficult otherwise to disentangle truth from vested interests. Posenenske, modular even in death, becomes who her commentators want her to be ("our bad conscience");[10] gallerists and curators and ex-husbands always have something to gain. We are left to examine our own pieties concerning a handful of ideas: that art making represents some kind of acme of engagement with "urgent social problems" rather than a salve, that it should operate parallel to political activism and should enact change at the same speed, that the artist has to be consistent, even, in their thinking. Contention is there, too, concerning where art stops—whether the category, if one was once an artist, arcs over the whole life. In its irresolution as narrative, Posenenske's portmanteau career keeps these issues in abiding play.

For a couple of decades, her work flickered intermittently in the art world. There was a survey in 1986 (the one at Maenz's gallery, her first solo showing since 1969) and a thin sprinkling of others up to 1990—including some installations set up by Brunn in fruit-and-vegetable markets, chemical factories, and art fairs that only ran a single day. During the 1990s, as art became increasingly characterized by precisely the type of interactive, audience-privileging strategies Posenenske pioneered, she was somehow nowhere. It was her work's reappearance in 2007's documenta 12, curated by Roger M. Buergel and Ruth Noack, that launched its widespread reappraisal, ironically so since one of Posenenske's final acts as an artist was to protest against the documenta 4 of 1968. There she involved herself in contrarian activities, for example, handing out flyers that pointed out how such exhibitions "blind us to social misery and the deplorable state of affairs in society."[11] (No mention was made of this, unsurprisingly, in the documenta 12 catalogue.)

From this point, amid an apotheosis of the art market that would surely have disgusted her, the cultural resurrection proceeded apace: gallery shows, retrospectives in Zurich, Paris, Antwerp, and New York, appearances in themed group exhibitions, a monograph. In 2010, at New York's Artists

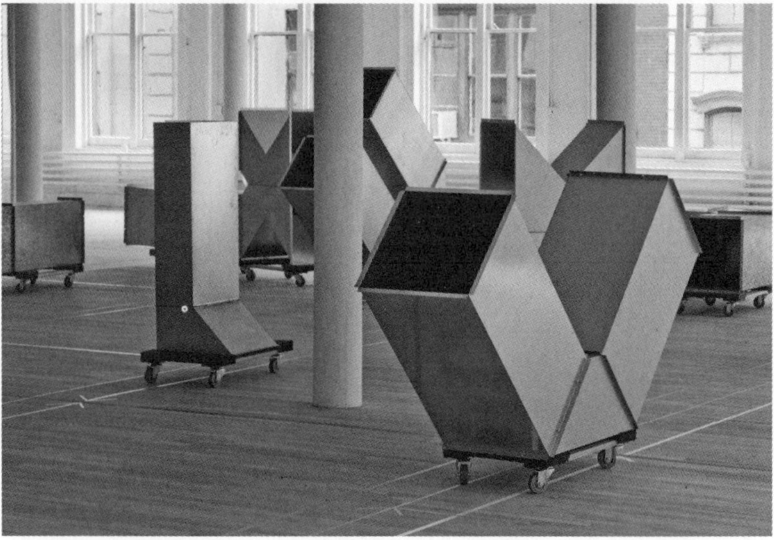

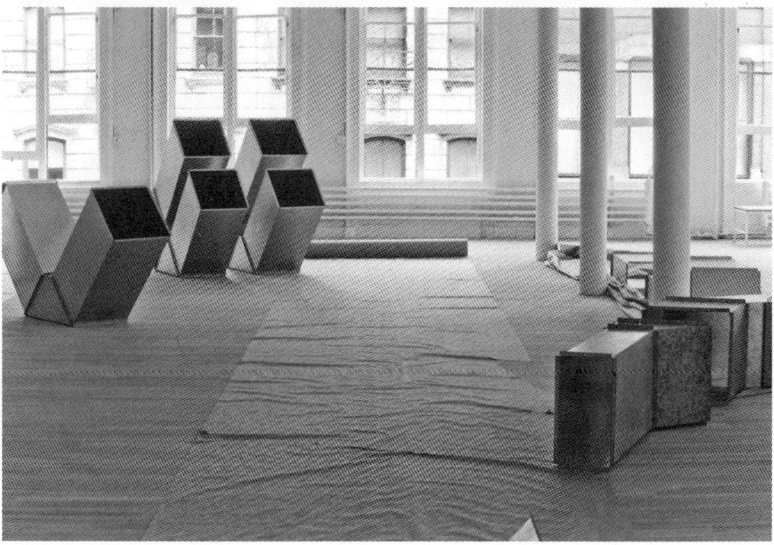

Charlotte Posenenske's *Square Tubes Series D*, 1967;
above: configured by Rirkrit Tiravanija, 2010;
below: configured by Ei Arakawa, 2010

Space—Posenenske's first US institutional solo—a different New York-based artist was invited every second weekend to reconfigure the work, including Rirkrit Tiravanija and Ei Arakawa. Here the "Square Tubes Series" were once more restyled: as cultural capital, as literal "connectors" between a late rediscovered refusenik—a distaff Bartleby—and another generation of relational practitioners, as romantic inspiration, as commodity. The venue republished Posenenske's sayonara to art in a booklet and on its website. "Though art's formal development has progressed at an increasing tempo, its social function has regressed," she had written forty-two years earlier.[12] Following this, she had stood outside the entrance to documenta handing out a broadside that read, in part, "You culture vultures, so here you are all gathered together to chat and lie and talk crap so as to gain the upper hand."[13] A small reception was held to mark each changeover of the New York show. Picture Charlotte Posenenske looking down, half-amused. Picture her looking away.

1. Burkhard Brunn, *Charlotte Posenenske (1930–1985): Erinnerungen an die Künstlerin* (Frankfurt am Main: Revolver, 2005), 119.
2. Christine Mehring, "Public Options: The Art of Charlotte Posenenske," *Artforum*, September 2010, 275.
3. Burkhard Brunn, "For an Introduction," in *Charlotte Posenenske*, ed. Museum für Moderne Kunst (Frankfurt am Main: Museum für Moderne Kunst, 1990), 5.
4. Cited in Christophe Cherix, ed., *In & Out of Amsterdam: Travels in Conceptual Art, 1960–1976* (New York: Museum of Modern Art, 2009), 108. Originally published in Charlotte Posenenske, *Art & Project Bulletin* 1 (September 1968).
5. Charlotte Posenenske, "Statements," *Art International* 12, no. 5 (May 1968): 50.
6. Cited in "Charlotte Posenenske an einem Bauunternehmer," *Egoist* 1 (1970): 17.
7. Mehring, "Public Options," 277.
8. Tellingly, Mehring translates it differently, more adamantly, as: "I find it difficult to accept that art cannot contribute to the solution of pressing social problems" (ibid., 273).
9. Brunn, "Biography," in *Charlotte Posenenske*, 79.
10. Mehring, "Public Options," 273.
11. Cited in Brunn, *Charlotte Posenenske (1930–1985)*, 117.
12. See http://artistsspace.org/exhibitions/charlotte-posenenske.
13. Cited in Brunn, *Charlotte Posenenske (1930–1985)*, 117.

Concepts of Distance

Photographs. In one, dating from Valentine's Day in 1964 and documenting a performance titled *I Have Hunger*, Stanley Brouwn stands before a small audience, wearing a suit, holding up a spoon and knife. Some kind of cord appears wrapped around his face, pinching and warping his features; a male onlooker looks disturbed, a woman amused. In another picture, taken the same day, the artist is clearly wearing wooden skis but otherwise his bent-over body is a blur. There are bottles on the ground and he's enacting, or making, something called *Brouwncocktail.* In a third image we see him in a crowd, over the shoulder of another man, a reel-to-reel tape recorder between them. Translating the image's Dutch caption clarifies that he's inviting guests at the opening of his exhibition at Galerie Patio, Neu-Isenburg, near Frankfurt, to speak into the machine, after which it'll be wrapped in clear plastic—as other photographs evidence—and their voices played back. In a fourth, a huge bunch of bananas appears to float before him while he holds an implement that looks, through the grainy monochrome murk, like a flyswatter. In a fifth he's on the ground, ringed by feet. There appears to be a magnifying glass at his side. He seems to be measuring something.

These photographs shouldn't exist. They were published in a slim book—a booklet, really—documenting the Dutch art scene of the period, a publication of whose every copy Brouwn apparently tried to destroy. (Outside of these and a handful of others in the same volume, only three or four images of him are in circulation.) Perhaps someone to whom I mentioned my interest in the artist shouldn't have skipped gleefully to the bookshelf, handing me something that had been kept hidden from Brouwn. Perhaps I shouldn't have taken out my iPhone like a microfilming spy. It's against the spirit of the work, which blurs with the life and professional decisions of a figure who virtually never consents to interviews and never, ever, to portraits; who has insisted since 1972 that no images of his work or biographical information be published (an exception, for documenta in that year, was laced with inaccuracies, misspelling his name and Paramaribo, his birthplace in Suriname); whose typical contribution to group

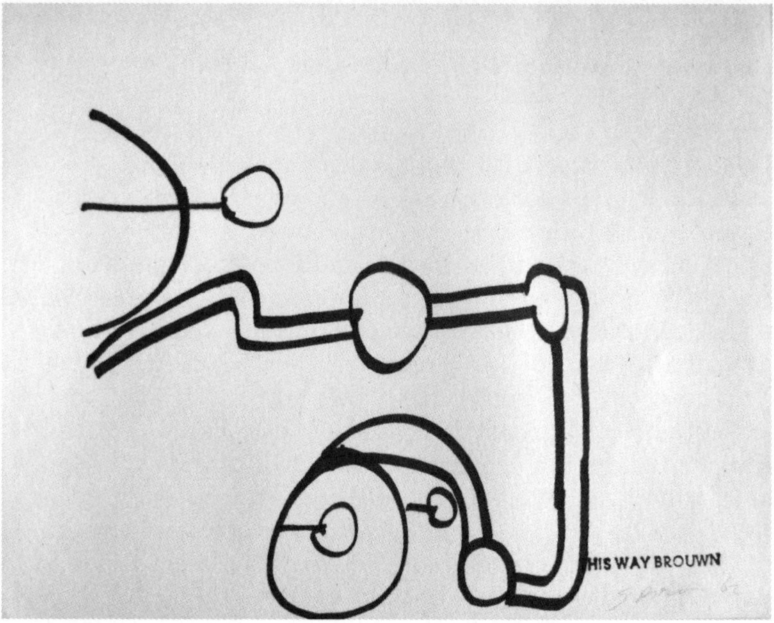

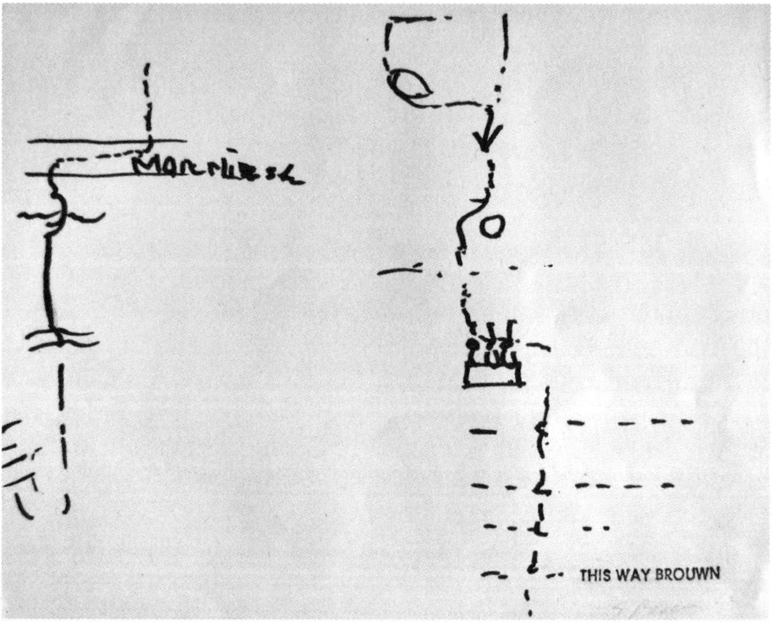

Stanley Brouwn, *This Way Brouwn*, 1960

exhibition catalogues is accordingly a blank page; and whose consummate vanishing into his art asks of his collaborators a "response" like that of his Berlin gallery, Konrad Fischer, when I first e-mailed to request that I might come in and look at their holdings of Brouwn's artist books. That is, pristine silence.

In the images, Brouwn—dark skin, professorial spectacles, big guileless eyes, receding close-cropped hair—is around twenty-nine years old. Seven years earlier, in 1957, he emigrated from Suriname, the tiny South American country and, at the time, Dutch colony, where he was born in 1935. The year of his arrival in Amsterdam, he appears on the radar, contributing a drawing and poem to the journal *Spiraal*, and features in the next four issues the following year. Somewhere around this time he makes his first (no longer extant) artwork, polyethylene bags filled with rubbish. Somewhere around this time, too, he connects—importantly, it would seem, for what he'll go on to do—to Nul, the Dutch cousin of the German ZERO group, which argued that art should be purged of color, feeling and individual expression. In 1960, as well as mailing out declarations that Amsterdam shoe stores are works of art by Stanley Brouwn, he initiates *This Way Brouwn* (1960–70). Still his best-known work and the first evidence of a will to displace authorship onto the audience, this is the start, too, of Brouwn's fascination with walking. For this project he asks passersby on the streets for directions and has them draw a map—each of these he stamps, like the refractory bureaucrat he has often been compared to, with the phrase "this way brouwn."

Two years later, Brouwn holds his first gallery show. A year after that, in 1963, he materializes on Dutch television in the arts program *View of a City in 24 Hours*, placing white paper sheets on the street for pedestrians to step on. Their footprints, their walking, make up the work—Brouwn lays the sheets, then returns later to gather them up. That same year he produces a different kind of focused defiling: a book, in an edition of one hundred, of pink silk tissue paper stained with lemon juice, the splotches only visible when heated. (Tragicomic apocrypha assert that, years later, a dealer trying to sell a rare copy is stymied when a cleaner, thinking it trash, throws it away.) Another book appears the following year, *Brouwnhairs* (1964)—seventy-six pages, a single hair of Brouwn's on each page—and a third, *BROUWNTOYS 4000 AD*, circa 1964. A 2014 photo spread for a feature by novelist-playwright Oscar van den Boogaard in *frieze* magazine reproduces two pages from the latter. On one, in violet capitals around a circle, is this:

> ENLARGE THE MICROBES AND VIRUSES IN
> THE CIRCLE 5000.000 TIMES.
> GIVE THEM TO YOUR CHILDREN TO PLAY WITH.

"Don't use the Brouwntoys before the year 4000 AD," Brouwn requests, or cautions. A half century on, as much as anything else, it is the idea, the cortical stretch achieved via language, of projecting a couple of millennia into the future that arrests me. For much of the rest of his career Brouwn will be beguiled by concepts of measure, by description as shorthand for extreme extension. He will use existing means of measurement, self-invented ones, arcane ones, and notions of travel, distance, and scale, as a way of increasing awareness of being in space, being with *others* in space, and, it would seem, communing with infinity. In Lucy R. Lippard's *Six Years: The Dematerialization of the Art Object from 1966 to 1972 ...* (1973) we find a description of a 1969 piece from a photolithographed bulletin published by Amsterdam gallery Art & Project, *Art and Project Bulletin 11: Prospect '69*. Below another bare circle is the sentence, laid out with poetical line breaks: "Walk during a few moments very consciously in a certain direction; simultaneously an infinite number of living creatures in the universe are moving in an infinite number of directions."[1]

Two years prior to this, in a rare interview—quoted by Van den Boogaard—Brouwn apparently said of *This Way Brouwn*, speaking in the third person as if he were an agency of sorts: "Brouwn makes people discover the streets they use every day. A farewell from the city, the earth, before we make the great leap into space, before we discover outer space."[2] It was 1967, a year before *2001: A Space Odyssey* and two before "Space Oddity," when space fever reigned, before the governmental space programs closed down. Five years before that, the first human had risen into orbit. Two years before, the first spacewalk. One year before, the first unmanned landing on another celestial body. Two years later, man on the moon. In the year of *BROUWNTOYS 4000 AD*, Brouwn composed a manifesto for the *Institute of Contemporary Arts Bulletin*:

4000 A.D.
When science and art are entirely
melted together to something new
When the people will have lost their
remembrance and thus will have
no past, only future.
When they will have to discover everything
every moment again and again
When they will have lost their need for
Contact with others ...
... Then they will live in a world of only
Colour, light, space, time, sounds and movement
Then colour light space time
sounds and movement will be free
No music
No theatre
No art
No
There will be sound
Colour
Light
Space
Time
Movement[3]

This is travel too, of course. As was Brouwn's *The Total Number of My Steps* (1972), for which, Christophe Cherix has written, "the artist planned consecutive trips in twenty-one cities, among them Oslo, Addis Ababa, Tokyo, and Dublin, which would be solely defined by the number of footsteps taken in each location."[4] In the longer *afghanistan–zambia* (1971) he indexed alphabetically the countries he planned to visit, leaving syntactical voids (e.g., "the total number of my steps in   monaco.")

Later, Brouwn would record his movements in cities, using a hand counter to tabulate them on index cards to be stored in metal filing cabinets. Later, too—from 1976 onward—he would not only use preexisting and self-invented divisions of distance, such as the SB-el, the SB-foot, and the SB-footstep, but also the ancient Egyptian—dating from 2500 BC—measurement of the royal cubit. (See, for example, his 1999 book *1 × 1 Royal Cubit*.)

In *Portraits of Spaces* (2001), published for a show at the Strasbourg Museum of Modern and Contemporary Art, Brouwn's idea of a "portrait" is to list the dimensions of the museum's rooms. A great deal of leeway is factored in; it intersects with precision and control.

Draw, in your mind's eye, a capacious circle. That might be Brouwn's work: at once theoretic and defined and with abundant space—for you, for anyone—in the middle, because apparent emptiness is never really empty, not when circumscribed as carefully as this. Yes, there is the grounding conceit of re-enchanting physical experience, against its dissolution by technology: a handful of quotes accredited to Brouwn in publicity materials for his 2005 exhibition at MACBA, in Barcelona, include the statement: "Never before have distances been so meaningless as nowadays. Increasingly more people fly long distance several times a year. The validity of the concept of distance is being still further eroded. In my work distances are recharged again. They regain meaning."[5] But then there's the question of what it means for meaningfulness to be restored to distance. So here's me, in the open tracts of Brouwn's work, and here's what it makes me think of.

In 1972, when the artist—who, to reiterate, hails from a former Dutch colony, one whose economy was founded on the slavery of Africans who were beaten, whipped, and starved, and that was hardly heavenly when Brouwn left in the 1950s—was planning his steps and thinking about space and (very probably) ancient Egypt, the African-American musician Sun Ra was making his film *Space Is the Place.* According to its plot, the sui generis jazz bandleader and his self-styled Arkestra left this planet in 1969 and settled on another one. Egyptology and sci-fi—here constituting a double movement away from a racist present, back to origins (however much the "black Egyptian" thesis has been questioned) and into the interstellar future—were a huge part of black nationalist culture in the 1960s and '70s, from Ra naming himself after the Egyptian god of the sun, to Earth Wind & Fire's populist takes on the same material, to funk bandleader George Clinton's regular invocations of space travel, the extraterrestrial mother ship as an upgraded low-swinging sweet chariot.

Meanwhile, in one 1970 exhibition entitled "Walking through Cosmic Rays," at the Städtisches Museum Abteiberg in Mönchengladbach, Germany, Brouwn refused to exhibit any art objects at all, so that viewers could experience the "cosmic rays"—debatable, this, since cosmic rays are high-velocity subatomic particles, radiation striking from space, that are supposed to only exist in the earth's upper atmosphere—in the building. (Sun Ra's own first band was called the Cosmic Rays.) A wall text read:

> how empty is this space?
> all the planets, thus including planet earth,
> constantly find themselves in a "shower" of cosmic rays
> in this space, as in every building on earth, it is also
> "raining cosmic rays"
> walking consciously through the invisible cosmic rays
> in this space confirms, intensifies
> the presence of this space

Brouwn has, so far as I know, never talked about these overlaps—again, for decades he has almost never spelled anything out—and it's purely a hypothesis, though with a certain amount of evidential propulsion. Consider *I Have Hunger*, which the artist would evidently rather we forgot; consider Cherix's neat summation that Brouwn's work conveys "a sense of inner travel that keeps the outside world at bay,"[6] or Van den Boogaard's "Brouwn is a space traveller and wants the viewers to become space travellers too."[7] Perhaps ask why the African-American artist David Hammons—whose work, as we'll see in the next chapter, is explicitly charged with racial issues while the artist himself determinedly remains, in many ways, removed from the art world—counts himself an admirer of Brouwn. Think of black and white: Brouwn diminishing himself in catalogues to the white page, or his acts that involve darkening something white—laying a brown hair on a white page in an artist's book; leaving white paper to be darkened with dirt. Think of Hammons's works involving darkening white sheets of paper with Harlem dirt from the surface of a thrown basketball. Think of Brouwn's identification with brown, both in a work like *Brouwnhairs* and elsewhere. (A video fragment reportedly exists of Jan Hoet, at Brouwn's 2001 exhibition opening at the SMAK in Ghent, talking to someone (one strongly suspects it's the artist) behind a pointedly brown wooden wall. The only brown aspect of a white space.)

Or think what you like—that this angle is reductive and tendentious and could be subsumed within a larger, more abstract idea of freedom from earthly restrictions. Or that it is always better to show than to tell. Do as you will with the fact that Brouwn so frequently contrasts an ostensibly real world with an idiosyncratic inward one, an actual unit of measure with a concocted surrogate, the physical experience of distance with the imagined and subjective and, tirelessly, the possibility of free movement, self-measure, self-governance, self-determination. His early publication *100 this-way-brouwn-problems for computer I. B. M. 360 model 95* (1970) found him writing mobility-related questions too big for a computer to deal with: "Show brouwn the way in all cities, villages, etc, on earth from point x to all other points in that cities, villages, etc."[8] A later work, *1 × 1 Foot* (1998), exemplifies his insistence on himself—or you—being the measure, comprising as it does a square drafted on the wall, dimensioned on the length of Brouwn's own foot. Moreover, that Brouwn's art even tempts such conjecture—about who gets to define scales, where to go, and how to get there—strewing periodic clues, is part of the structural appeal and functional paradox of his working method. The last Brouwn solo exhibition I saw was in 2012, at Konrad Fischer. It featured some framed diagrammatic works and axial measurements on the floor. The sense of spaciousness, even by conceptual art criteria, was extraordinary: short texts envisioning immense distances, gargantuan numbers. (A parallel figure in this regard was, of course, On Kawara, whose ostensibly conceptual work has also been viewed as backed by large-scale trauma.) The work spurs as it withdraws, as its maker recedes.

And perhaps you're exhorted enough that you begin asking around, guiltily, despite yourself. How awkward and conflicted you feel about this might clarify, in turn, how far Brouwn operates in contradistinction to a mass-media and now social-media age of absolute transparency—how far you're watermarked by it. You discover that Brouwn, in person—for he's not exactly a recluse but also a parent who taught for many years at a postgraduate

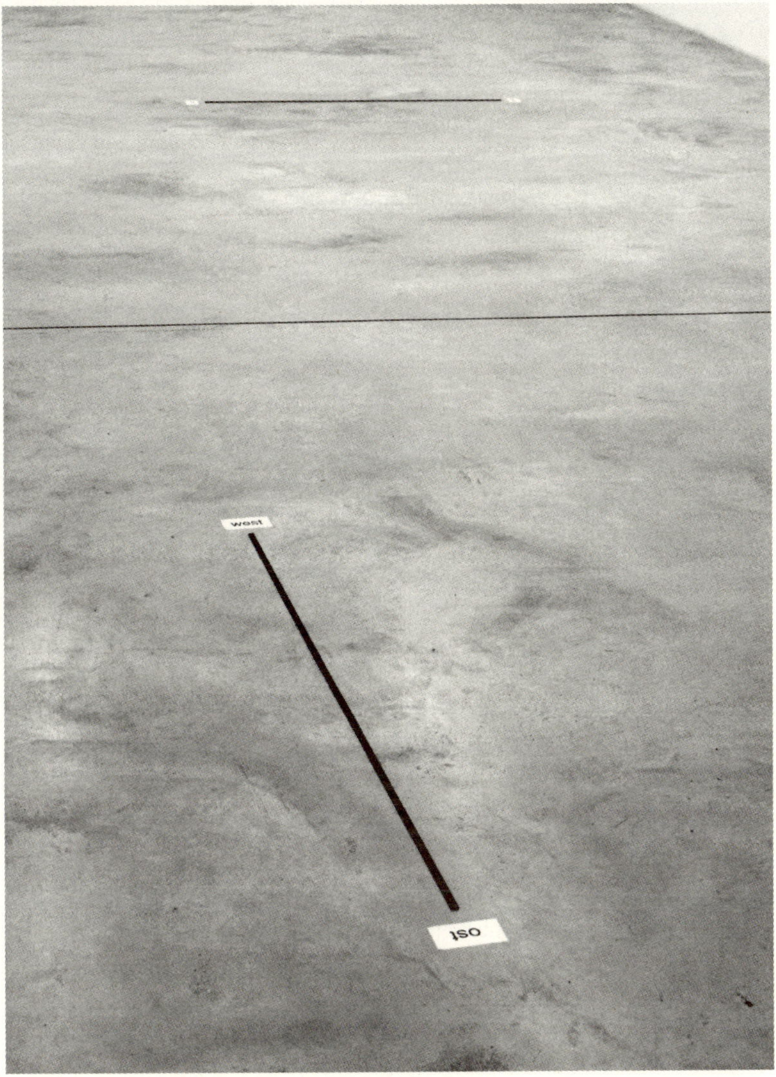

Stanley Brouwn, *in diesem moment gehen x personen auf dem alexanderplatz in berlin in richtung norden. in diesem moment gehen x personen auf dem alexanderplatz in berlin in richtung süden*, 2012

art academy in Amsterdam and, prior to that, in Germany—is garrulous, but in a fitting way. He asks lots of questions, of the what-did-you-have-for-breakfast variety. He's curious, but seemingly in a manner that deflects attention away from him, just as does his displacing art, with its early attention—prefiguring a major shift in this direction in the 1990s—toward the viewer's constructive subjectivity. You hear that when venerable Italian gallerist Massimo Minini visits, Brouwn insists on meeting in one café in Amsterdam Centraal train station. You hear from someone else that that's very likely true, because Brouwn loves train stations. You decide, on a whim, to type "Stanley Brouwn interview" into YouTube—akin to searching for televised fireside chats with Thomas Pynchon—and you're highly surprised to find something; a seventy-second snippet of telephone chatter dated January 31, 2014, presumably recorded clandestinely and invasively and unseen/heard by Brouwn. (This, of course, connotes the difference between our world and the one that existed when Brouwn electively dropped out.) When you find this upload it has been viewed only fifty-five times. Brouwn's voice is high and friendly. He laughs. Half against your better judgment, you have it translated; and here—having surged across your own line, established what constitutes violation—you quit snooping, quit asking.

❀

In 1970, a year after Kawara inaugurated his two-million-year spanning (one million into the past, one million into the future) *One Million Years* (1969), Brouwn published his first artist's book, the thirty-two page *Tatvan* (also known as *x-Tatwan*). He had ventured to the eponymous mountain town in eastern Turkey—where the railway ends, to avoid cutting through hilly terrain—to photograph the route of what could be a railway extension. Cast this in metaphorical terms. Brouwn seemingly wanted to photograph the idea of a journey that couldn't yet be made, but someday might. Instead he decided not to include the images in the book—while, it seems, making the refusal public—and recorded instead, on successive pages, the cumulative distance from various unknown locations (all listed as "x") to Tatvan, including:

x – Tatwan 1000 000 000 000 000 000 000 000 000 000 000 000 000 000 000 000 000

One and fifty-one zeroes: a sexdecillion miles if the measurement is, indeed, in miles (the volume of the Milky Way has been estimated at a sexdecillion cubic miles). The x might be you, roaming ever further from the intolerable real. A journey of a thousand miles, Lao-tzu famously wrote, starts with the first step: Brouwn insists that the first step in whatever distance is always in your head, including the class of measure; and to expedite your own step, his own movement has been resolutely away from us. Try the thought experiment that Brouwn *doesn't* withdraw—that he accepts interviews, that he's asked why he uses the royal cubit, why distance, why this, why that. The refusals, care, and control feel indivisible from the work—are a performative aspect that never stopped but only slipped into the negative. At one end of the spectrum is Stanley Brouwn in 1964, in public, bound and hungry or crawling on the floor. At the other end, somewhere, is Stanley Brouwn today. Measure, if you please, the empty space between. How full it is.

1. Cited in Lucy R. Lippard, *Six Years: The Dematerialization of the Art Object from 1966 to 1972 …* (London: Studio Vista, 1973), 115.
2. Cited in Oscar van den Boogaard, "In Search of Stanley Brouwn," *frieze*, March 2014, 122.
3. Stanley Brouwn, "Manifesto 4000 A. D.," in *Bloomsday 1964* (Frankfurt: Galerie Loehr, 1964), unpaginated.
4. Christophe Cherix, *In & Out of Amsterdam: Travels in Conceptual Art, 1960–1976* (New York: Museum of Modern Art, 2009), 21.
5. Cited in the press release for exhibition "Stanley Brouwn," MACBA, Barcelona, 2005.
6. Cherix, *In & Out of Amsterdam*, 20.
7. Van den Boogaard, "In Search of Stanley Brouwn," 122.
8. Stanley Brouwn, *100 this-way-brouwn-problems for computer I. B. M. 360 model 95* (Cologne: Verlag Gebr. König, 1970), unpaginated.

Street Level

Toward the end of 2014, David Hammons presented a survey of works from the last dozen years at London's White Cube gallery. That's the correct way of putting it: the venue may have been London's biggest homegrown dealership, but Hammons—at that time, though quietly, the eighth most expensive living American artist—heavily outranked it. Usually, as we know, the seesaw is balanced differently: artists desire and pursue representation and big institutional shows. Hammons has mostly scorned both for decades, preferring to sell out of his studio or, more recently, through auctioneers (the previous year, he'd auctioned a single work for eight million US dollars). Usually, too, the gallery takes half the profits. For the White Cube show, which opened in the privileged calendar slot coincident with Frieze Art Fair, the artist who in 2002 told critic Peter Schjeldahl that "the Whitney Biennial and Documenta need me, but I don't need them,"[1] was said to have negotiated a 90/10 split.

Hammons elected on this occasion to further salt the pot by showing one work he had exhibited with the same gallery twelve years before, in a little project-space show apparently agreed to as a favor to guest curator Louise Neri. *Traveling* (2002) is a large sheet of paper against which Hammons had repeatedly slammed a basketball previously bounced, so he claimed, along Harlem's dusty pavements. The result was a velvety cloud-like abstraction, and behind the propped frame was a leather suitcase pointing to mobility and self-sufficiency. (The title, typical of Hammons's double-dealing approach, also refers to an illegal basketball move.) In 2014 Hammons surrounded this archival work with a bunch of cool variations on the same, newly made, that whiffed strongly of product. He additionally presented variants on pieces he'd shown in two previous exhibitions since 2007 at blue-chip gallery L&M Arts on New York's Upper East Side (where he had hired the ritzy venue out of his own pocket, using it as what the *New York Times* called "a kind of stage").[2] A fur coat was splashed and daubed with paint; Abstract Expressionist-style canvases were covered, frustratingly though in a latter-day trademark fashion, with grimy tarps. Some of the gallery's architectural features were removed—a pointedly symbolic exposure. (That another artist shortly before had done something similar in the same venue didn't seem to trouble Hammons.) Hung in an anteroom, notably, was a little drawing by Agnes Martin.

The totality was, even as a purported recap, outwardly a little disappointing, overfamiliar, latently commerce-minded. And yet Hammons, who once called the overwhelmingly white, status-obsessed, hermetic art world "the worst audience in the world," may well have intended it that way.[3] He could have put up this commercial show, with its reminders of urban realities and inequalities, and taken the money and run. Maybe he did. But it's quite possible that all of this, beyond its scuzzy critical presence in the ritzy purlieu of Mayfair, was in the service of something hard to criticize.

Several months before his London show, Hammons had bought—for just over two million dollars—a property in Yonkers, New York: a one-story warehouse he announced he was planning to renovate as an exhibition space. (He had, indeed, begun talking about plans to do such a thing as early as 1993, so a catalogue text from that time attests.) When this news was revealed, the move into gallery sales—which had puzzled long-term watchers of an artist who, since the latter part of the 1970s, often preferred to work directly on the street, bypassing an art audience for an urban constituency—made a bit more sense. It was recast, if one brackets off Hammons's theatrical swipes at the luxury market from within, as a mustering in the services of further autonomy, one whose credo might have come from James Brown's 1974 "Funky President (People It's Bad)": "Put up your factory and own the job."

The Yonkers building was purchased under the company name Duchamp Realty LCC, a fact that rewinds us through Hammons's career. For you'd look lengthily to find an artist more in sync with Marcel Duchamp's analytic owning of the art world as a system, rather than being owned by it, and this has been the case for decades now. Hammons's relationship to Duchamp, though, is complex and indicative, involving the former publicly taking what he needs: using Duchamp's language and the language of conceptual, anti-"retinal" art that descends from him emphatically to his own ends. While Hammons once positioned himself "somewhere between Marcel Duchamp, Outsider art and *Arte Povera*,"[4] to Schjeldahl he wryly bemoaned the Frenchman's influence, and this makes sense too.[5]

Specifically, since the late 1960s Hammons has used modernist negation and Dadaist uproar in dialogical ways that keep his art at street level and oxygenated with critique, rather than reified in a museum, further enriching the rich, assuaging status anxiety, and preaching liberal pieties to the choir. But his unimpeachable daylight raids on the gallery system in the twenty-first century also represent the closing of a circle, a tactical return to a world Hammons had abandoned three decades earlier. He had been processed, relatively smoothly, through the system once before.

✽

Born in Springfield, Illinois, in 1943, Hammons left for Los Angeles at age twenty, studied advertising and then art (at Otis College of Art and Design and Chouinard Art Institute, which would become CalArts), and, in the emergent context of black nationalism, began in his mid-twenties making politically charged works: body prints of his own and other black bodies that took off on Yves Klein's *Anthropometries* from a decade or so before. (This would not be Hammons's last engagement with Klein.) The prints, which Hammons made until the early 1970s by coating flesh, clothing, and even headgear with grease (e.g., margarine), pressing them against paper, and dusting the impression with pigment, injected race concerns into contemporary art dialogue—they sometimes involved the American flag as a symbol of broken promises to African-Americans—and more generally held up a mirror to black audiences. Presented here were literal brutal traces of hard-knock experience: the two men, Hammons upfront, drinking from a brown-bagged bottle in *The Wine Leading the Wine* (1969), for example; the figure tied to a chair in *Injustice Case* (1970).

Yet Hammons, who has noted that in Los Angeles he inhabited a peer context where exhibiting often was frowned upon, appears to have become quickly frustrated by the art object as commodity. His body prints, while mostly framed, on occasion fragmented, turned temporary: see *Black Boy's Window* (1968), a body print on a window with a blind that could be raised or lowered. In the early '70s, he walked away from what had become a signature style and began working with assemblage, partly following increased awareness of Duchamp, but also after looking at figures such as Dadaist/funk assemblage artists Noah Purifoy and John Riddle, who both made work from the detritus of the 1965 Watts riots in Los Angeles. The compound objects Hammons began fashioning now were at once aesthetically low and conceptually watertight. A series of works using spades, beginning with painting and moving into sculpture (see *Spade with Chains*, 1973, in which chains—themselves, of course, a contextually loaded material—hung from an inverted shovel create a semiabstract tribal mask) on one level refer back to the Duchamp of *In Advance of the Broken Arm* (1915), the snow-shovel readymade. They also probe Hammons's own admitted confusion about a racial insult: "I was trying to figure out why black people were called spades, as opposed to clubs. Because I remember being called a spade once, and I didn't know what it meant."[6] Hammons acted out violence on his shovels: he hung them from trees, ran them over; for *Bird* (1973), referencing the nickname of bebop genius Charlie Parker, he plunged a spade's handle into a saxophone's neck.

These were rhetorically powerful proposals and they haven't dated at all. In the mid-'70s, though, around the time he moved to New York, Hammons began transitioning. His materials started to come straight from the streets, specifically those of black neighborhoods. For his 1975 show "Greasy Bags and Barbecue Bones," held at Just Above Midtown Gallery, a space dedicated to black artists, Hammons fashioned assemblages and mobiles out of the leftovers of black culture: hair, carefully grease-stained brown paper bags, the bones of spareribs. Hammons would continue working with these gratis materials, more baroquely, for the rest of the decade. Consider the lyrical but troubled *Hair and Wire, Venice Beach* (1977), in which baubles of black hair stick to swaying coat-hanger wires embedded in sand. In his use of them one observes a philosophy.

Not incidentally, such materials—barbershop sweepings, food detritus—not only contained the afterglow of life lived but were also free. Unhitching yourself from costs, controlling the means of production, unshackling yourself from crippling overheads: these, Hammons has said, constitute a route to artistic freedom, one to which he has doggedly stuck. In Los Angeles Hammons had a big but very cheap studio, in New York he famously lived above a fried-chicken outlet; even his favorite activity, walking the city, is costless and in turn has repeatedly given him artistic ideas. Nothing is wasted. His art boils bones to make a rich stock. It plays off the very fact that his materials are dirty, not *valued*, and what a process leaves behind. See, perhaps most transformatively, a work like *Elephant Dung Sculpture* (1978), a balled elephant dropping ringed with colorful paint and gold leaf, waste material turned into a miniature icon of Africa.

But Hammons in this period went further than drawing materialist energies from the sidewalk. He also returned to it, showing an increasing interest in an unmediated address that bypassed galleries and all they stand for; an address that sometimes even operated, after the fact, merely as ungraspable rumor. As the '70s went on, he began placing installations of hair, bottle caps salvaged from bars, and fried-chicken bones in vacant lots in Harlem. In 1981 he made *Pissed Off*, a performance (captured in a series of photographs by Dawoud Bey) in which he urinated on Richard Serra's imposing steel-plate sculpture *T.W.U.* (1980–81), an implicit commentary on the socially disengaged nature of formalist sculpture. (The same year, in the undocumented performance *Shoe Tree*, Hammons tossed twenty-five pairs of sneakers over the same sculpture.) In the winter of 1983, close to the Cooper Union art school in the East Village, he made *Bliz-aard Ball Sale*, his infamous sporadic sales (or single sale, depending who you ask) of variously sized and priced snowballs (or equally priced, depending again who you ask) that suggested anything white is valuable—a work that loops complexly on itself, since it also situates Hammons as a trickster figure who can sell melting snow. The lesser-known *Doll Shoe Salesman* (1985), not ephemeral but equally pinned to the purchasable useless, was never documented.

Alongside these samizdat affairs, though again pursuing situations unmediated by the gallery system, Hammons began

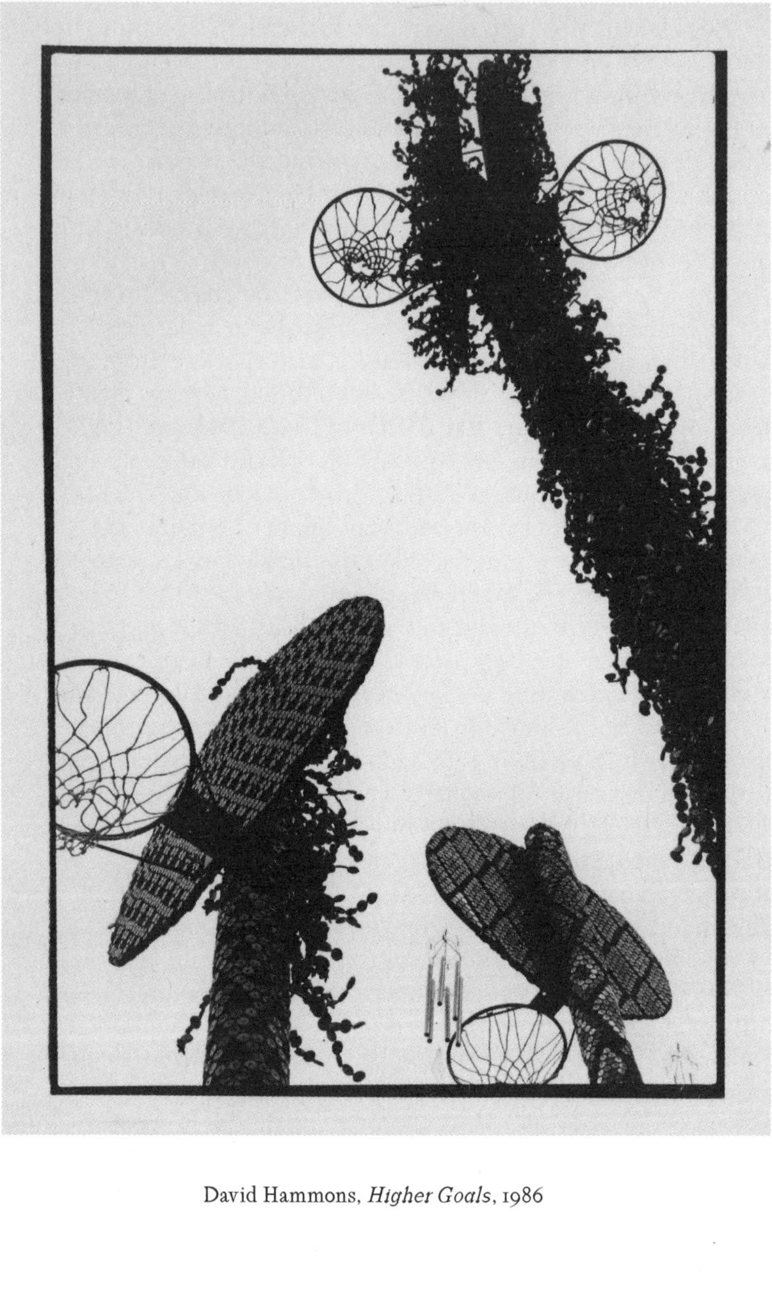

David Hammons, *Higher Goals*, 1986

working on more official outdoor and public commissions. In 1980 the series of delicate assemblages mordantly entitled "Flight Fantasy" (1978–83), amalgams of hair and paper bags and glitter, made their way into various bays at Atlanta airport. For *Higher Goals* (1986), sited in Brooklyn's Cadman Plaza Park when he was artist-in-residence for the Public Art Fund, Hammons—who had grown up with hoop dreams but, to his chagrin, stopped growing physically—appliquéd a quintet of twenty- to thirty-foot-high telephone poles with used beer-bottle caps and crowned them with unreachable basketball hoops and backboards. The work thus operated a double critique: of a culture that limited black youth's ambitions to sports stardom, and of the selfsame black youth who didn't dream of anything but fame and money.

That year, in one of his already infrequent interviews (they've since dwindled to zero), Hammons rationalized his preference for public viewership. The art audience, he said, is "overly educated, it's conservative, it's out to criticize and not to understand, and it never has any fun. Why should I spend my time playing to that audience?"[7] Though the street audience could also misunderstand. Not everyone, for example, "got" *How Ya Like Me Now?* (1988), Hammons's Kool Moe Dee–quoting image of Jesse Jackson with blue eyes, blond hair, and a white face on a billboard in Washington, DC, which was attacked with sledgehammers by enraged black citizens. The work came inside, and indeed Hammons's work continued to come inside, generally inside institutions, in group shows.

Hammons, by this point, had long detached himself from the art world's machinations. He had discovered that if you run they'll run after you; that although the art world considers itself the top of the credibility tree, its highest branch is reserved for the figure who can play its games and still disdain it. He positioned himself there. Asking how he did it, one might begin by suggesting that few artists have Hammons's taste for economy and even less his capacity for the razor-sharp, brilliantly timed and positioned gesture (or his patience). Not many, either, have so smartly put into play what Christian Haye and Coco Fusco, in an excellent 1995 analysis, characterized as the practice of "signifyin'," theorized by literary critic Henry Louis Gates: "Signifyin', according to Gates, involves taking, twisting and transforming English to make it otherwise. It implicitly revindicates 'imitation' as a creative gesture, over and against a legacy of negative, Eurocentric appraisal of black literature and culture as unoriginal. To signify is to rework received meanings; the difference between the literal and the metaphorical is thrust into the foreground by an approach that operates by implication, indirect communication, imagistic rendering, rhythmic delivery, and parody."[8]

The signifyin' approach allows Hammons to be influenced (by Dada and Klein, for instance) yet to twist the influence, blacken it, pastiche it, own it. In terms of differentiation this links to his approach to handiwork. Repeatedly, he's spoken of his admiration for how he perceives black artisanship, carpentry for example, which is reflected in his own sculptural handiwork: not perfectly—everything a tiny bit off, behind the beat—but it feels right. (A 2010 exhibition at the Studio Museum in Harlem, "30 Seconds Off an Inch," even quoted Hammons's approval of the same in its title.) If such an approach, mobilized in his own art, was aimed at the black community, it also shows up the white one as capsuled by the art world—its pieties, staleness, safeness. At the same time, the art community loves to be tickled, as the accommodation of institutional critique into institutions themselves has proved. And it needs, seemingly, an embodiment of its guilty conscience. These aspects, alongside his extraordinary visual/conceptual intelligence, have helped propel Hammons. While they might disgust him, they offer a context whose ugliness, too, folds dialectically into his art, something else to rise above and to analyze, over and over, in order to put the opposition in check.

❀

One might, amid all of this, identify three broad shifts in Hammons's career. (A fourth, in which he shores up his legacy—perhaps because his invisibility has served him a little too well—might be afoot: this may be another reason for the gallery shows, which in 2016 extended to a fifty-year career survey at New York's Mnuchin Gallery, and for the in-progress institution.) First, operating within commercial galleries. Second, ditching them for settings in which his work would reach the black audiences it was primarily made for (like city streets or black boutiques). Third, reengaging with the commercial realm while toting a new agenda—albeit one that may volte-face again—to hide things from whites, to hold something back, and to do so in the language of abstraction—the opposite, arguably, of the language of representation to which black art had previously (with notable exceptions such as the work of Jack Whitten and Frank Bowling) primarily gravitated. Abstraction here would become synonymous with a controlled absence, with not seeing something. Though such a denial might be considered in another way: as Bowling wrote in his 1971 essay "It's Not Enough to Say 'Black Is Beautiful,'" "the traditional esthetic of black art, often considered pragmatic, uncluttered and direct, really hinges on secrecy and disguise."[9]

If the tendency first appeared within Hammons's art back in 1969 with *Black Boy's Window*, then a hinge work in this regard—following a decade in which he did not assent to a New York gallery show—was *Concerto in Black and Blue* (2002–03), which took an existing trope descending from Klein's all-white empty gallery *The Void* (1958) and placed it in negative. Blacking out the lights of Doug Christmas's cavernous Ace Gallery in New York, Hammons offered visitors tiny blue flashlights to navigate with (the specific shade another reference to Klein, specifically his International Klein Blue). Here was not a white cube but a black cube,[10] here was a title with overtones of jazz but also of a bruising beating, here was blackness as anxiety and also a refusal of vision—a negation of art's core register, the visible. Even before he began ramping up this refusal, though, Hammons was saying no on other levels. Aside from his aversion to interviews, he doesn't show up at parties, he doesn't work the circuit; indeed, he revels in being difficult, in royally fucking with potential interlocutors. What the art world can take from him, in terms of his presence, is fiercely and actively attenuated. It is, as with other artists in this book, plausibly an extension of the work.

In 1996 I stood in Chris Ofili's London studio listening to a Sun Ra CD and to the painter as he spoke about his admiration for Hammons—admiration that anyone familiar with Ofili's early work would recognize, since the latter constituted a transparent shout-out. *Shithead*, made three years before, could have been a Hammons: it comprised dreadlocks set into a globe of elephant dung. *Shit Sale*, presented the year before that, found Ofili setting up stalls in street markets in East London and Berlin to sell balls of African elephant dung obtained from Whipsnade Zoo. Ofili would soon go on to apply globes of dung to his canvases, his nod to Hammons just one of many to Afrocentric culture in his art. I asked him why he thought more artists didn't act like Hammons, why the attention economy made them so terrified. Ofili said he didn't know, but a larger, subtler tribute to Hammons on his part would come nine years later when he upped sticks to Trinidad—where his work began, rewardingly, to change—started refusing interviews, and began only intermittently returning for his own openings.[11] The trajectory was familiar. An artist goes through the system, receives recognition, steps away from it, and starts operating increasingly on his own terms. Meanwhile, as he leans back, the art industry leans, as if magnetized, toward him.

Hammons himself is as much a linkage, as is Ofili, in a daisy chain of influence, one that has black and white artists in it. See Duchamp's withdrawal-cum-"retirement." See Hammons's pointed inclusion in his White Cube show of that little Agnes Martin drawing. See also Stanley Brouwn, who Hammons apparently admires—another figure who began in the gallery, then moved out onto the street. In a 2010 exhibition at MoMA, Brouwn's *Steps of Pedestrians on Paper* (1960) was hung opposite Hammons's *Untitled (Kool-Aid)* (2003). In the former work, unknowing passersby did the composing: the result was somewhere between Tom Sawyer getting other kids to whitewash his fence (though all here is turning black, not white), and Hammons lusciously covering sheets of paper with, obstensibly, Harlem dirt from a tossed basketball. This led one back to think about Brouwn's purposeful evasiveness: his refusal of interviews, or of his own physical presence in the art system.

Hammons's own piece, facing it, also put the onus of effort on someone other than a black artist. It constitutes a drawing that glows pink beneath a diaphanous white silk veil: a "keep out" marker recalling how both "dirty" pictures and Buddhist sutras were once covered by curtains, and a denial that stretches back from Hammons's own work through histories of signifyin' and black slang to Charlie Parker and his compatriots inventing harmonic extensions and playing at fearsome speeds in order to keep outsiders off the bandstand. To see what was beneath, the viewer of *Untitled (Kool-Aid)* had to make an appointment, then turn up at a time decided by the artist—only a few minutes each week—and enter the institution through a different entrance.

Of course people signed up, resisting refusal, chasing something they thought might be special or anticipating, perhaps, a crafty disappointment. What they got was beautiful but tinctured with deep unease, a pink abstraction made with the eponymous drink—notorious, of course, as the vessel for poison drunk by over nine hundred blindly obedient followers of the Reverend Jim Jones in 1978—and stamped with the logo of the Kool-Aid Man. David Hammons, meanwhile, was miles away, thinking about something else.

1. Cited in Peter Schjeldahl, "The Walker: Rediscovering New York with David Hammons," *New Yorker*, December 23, 2002, http://www.newyorker.com/magazine/2002/12/23/the-walker.
2. Holland Cotter, "The Upper East Side Goes Grungy in David Hammons's Gallery Show," *New York Times*, March 1, 2011, http://www.nytimes.com/2011/03/02/arts/design/02hammons.html.
3. David Hammons, cited in Kellie Jones, "David Hammons" (1986), *REALLIFE Magazine: Selected Writings and Projects 1979–1994*, ed. Miriam Katzeff, Thomas Lawson, and Susan Morgan (New York: Primary Information, 2006), 236–43.
4. Hammons, cited in Kellie Jones, "The Structure of Myth and the Potency of Magic," in *David Hammons: Rousing the Rubble* (New York: Institute for Contemporary Art, 1991), 29.
5. "I'm the C.E.O. of the D. O. C.—the Duchamp Outpatient Clinic. We have a vaccine for that smartness virus that's been in the art world for the last fifty years." Hammons, cited in Schjeldahl, "The Walker."
6. David Hammons, "Interview with David Hammons," by Kellie Jones, in *EyeMinded: Living and Writing Contemporary Art* (Durham, NC: Duke University Press, 2011), 249.
7. Ibid., 255–56.
8. Coco Fusco and Christian Haye, "Wreaking Havoc on the Signified," *frieze*, May 1995, http://www.frieze.com/article/wreaking-havoc-signified.
9. Frank Bowling, quoted in "Reciprocal Gestures: Mark Godfrey on Melvin Edwards and Frank Bowling in Dallas," *Artforum*, May 2015, 100.
10. Indeed, consider that Hammons had his first White Cube show at the same time, and that he might even have partly chosen that gallery for the uneasy resonance of its name.
11. Looking at Ofili's latter-day works using deep, almost unreadable shades of blue and black paint, one might consider his admiration for Hammons still evident in his work.

Here and Not Here

A few pages into Lutz Bacher's 2008 artist's book *SMOKE (gets in your eyes)*, there's a photocopy image of a square sheet, maybe a napkin, with two columns of words handwritten on it. "Lute Bateau," it reads, then "Klutz Backer." The mutations continue, the artist's unknown real name vanishing behind variations on her long-standing pseudonym. On the next page is a triplicate definition of "Lutz": evidently this could mean a few things, including the pet form of Ludwig, and derives from German or French. Soon after, in a reproduced e-mail, someone (name redacted) tries to define what is "Lutzian": qualities ranging from "moments of particular social rupture or awkwardness" to "bizarre behaviour in general, particularly around women" to "moral horror." Paging on, we find a curator writing to the artist after watching twelve hours of videotaped interviews in which Bacher asks artists, framers, and gallerists to describe her: "As if, after all those hours, I still believed there was such a thing as *knowing* you." Many such conversations are transcribed in a 2012 book titled (like the video work) *Do You Love Me?*,[1] replete with attention-derailing ums and typos—a generous self-exposure that isn't exposure at all, rather a cortege of chaos. Here and not here, c'est Lutz.

I'm looking at the handful of online photographs of her, taken at private views, where she's always dressed in black. In some she's covering her face, in others she doesn't bother. I talk to one of her gallery directors about interviewing her. He says sometimes she will, sometimes she won't. I don't pursue it; he tells me some things—her age, a recent bereavement—that are enough, too much already. He hands me the galleys of Bacher's next book, *SHIT FOR BRAINS* (2015), a wayward, confessional, fearless little "novel" she handwrote on A4 sheets in 2010, leaving in the crossings-out. It reads as puked up quick from the heart and yet issued out of absence.

Here and not here has been Bacher's modus operandi since the mid-1970s. Her approach has been to constantly shape-shift, deny her authorial signature, disperse like smoke. Back in 1976/77—years when her gender was unrevealed—she worked with both found and self-produced photography, artist's books, interviews, video, performance. Her artworks barely resembled each other: *Men at War* (1975) comprises cropped photographs of groups of men "whose central figure wears both a US Navy cap & a swastika painted on his chest"; in *The Milk Video* (1976), "a man had a dream where I was drinking a glass of milk";[2] *Standard Stoppage* (1976) offers blurry photographs of a tree; in *Documents of Rape* (1977), snapshots and diagrams anatomize a possible sexual assault. Several things are going on in this nexus of proposals. A pluralistic approach, au courant during the 1970s but peculiarly fitting and instrumentalized in Bacher's case; a nod to Marcel Duchamp's chance-driven work *3 Standard Stoppages* (1913–14) that might also salute Duchamp's own gender fluidity (as Rrose Sélavy) and post-medium elusiveness; a complex of thoughts around masculinity and male power, from soldiers to dreamed-of "milk" drinking to rape. In the midst of this, there's an artist who, as her willful aesthetic already signals, will not be possessed or processed.

After this sequence of works—reproduced in Bacher's chronological 2013 catalogue *SNOW*—she melts away for five years, appearing to produce nothing at all. Whatever the actual reason, such structural absences scan as concordant with her practice. The "work" itself is composed partly of art objects, partly of an enigmatic performative aspect, and all of this, in turn, is a meditation on the self. "A biography is considered complete if it merely accounts for six or seven selves, whereas a person may well have as many thousand," writes Virginia Woolf in *Orlando* (1928).[3] Bacher's biography, if she plays this game to the hilt, may never be considered complete. This, after all, is the artist who, in 2008, made *BINGO (or the year I was born)*, a bingo sign with numbers programmed to light up in random sequences. Even if you didn't care when Bacher was born—you can find various dates online spanning from 1945 to 1954—or what her real name is, she continues to point to the fact that she's not telling.

❀

If you want to be systematic about the artworks she has made, though, they'll permit that to an extent. They often vouchsafe

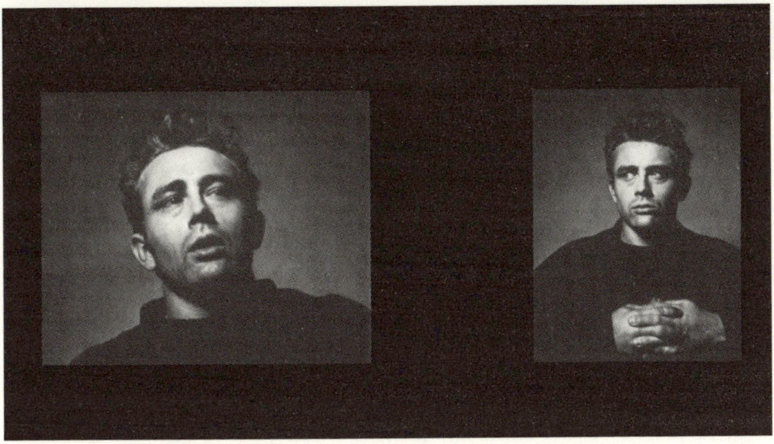

Lutz Bacher, still from video slide show, *James Dean*, 1986

an aesthetics of betweenness, of conscious undecidedness. Consistencies arise only to implode later; where variation appears to rule, links will ultimately appear. Consider *James Dean* (1986), which cross-fades slide images of the fabled actor. In one he's looking right; in another, left. No one view is more definitive, plus the image itself is destabilized. It stands for more than a set of publicity shots, opening onto some uncharted, ambiguously metaphoric realm. Preexisting images, Bacher has repeatedly averred, are not *fixed*. People aren't either.

So the media image becomes the readymade, which comes to lose its initial semiotic sense, which blows it open, which makes it, in turn, analogical. Specifically, this process engages gender concerns, then capsules them within the problem of typologies and their relation to power. In the series "Jokes" (1987–88), unconnected obscene captions are applied to journalistic photos. (Jane Fonda is seen to say, at a press conference, "I'm really weird. I'm really all fucked up.") In *Sex with Strangers* (1986), blown-up black-and-white porn images pair with captions from "a sexually explicit paperback written in the mode of a sociological study."[4] Liz Kotz, in a 1992 article for *Artforum*, writes that the captions, "in their lurid accounts of female nymphomania and wayward hitchhikers, veer between voyeurism, parody, and the faux-scientific tone that lends vintage porn its campy tenor." They "fail to 'anchor' the images," she continues, sending them spinning out of control.[5] Bacher's occupation with images by men, for women, meanwhile, creates a sphere of fertile ambivalence, and also suggests that the fixity of gender roles is the problem and the best thing to do, via a rewiring of the gaze, is to detonate it.

She continues, for a while, to routinely take up roles typically assigned to men and to work with masculinity, domination, self-defense. See *Playboys* (1991–94), paintings and drawings based on illustrations from the men's magazine; numerous concurrent works connected to rape and child abuse, like male adult anatomical dolls; *Shooter* (1993), a video of Bacher discharging handguns. Fugue-like, though, maleness is subsequently de-emphasized—it will flare up again, at later points—and replaced by other stresses. Child abuse segues, in disturbing ways, into childhood (which had briefly reared its head in *Mechanical Reproduction*, 1983, a progressive enlargement of a photograph of a baby) and the psychology of the parent-child relationship. (*Talk to Me*, 1994, is a pink sack "that contains a foetus.")[6] Then this in turn recedes. For several years, Bacher appears focused on observational and documentary video that either makes her an invisible flaneuse or deflects attention. But in 2005 she cycles back, making works featuring trolls and boys in pilots' uniforms and incubators and pregnant mannequins. Even change, she suggests, can be reversed upon lest it be recognized as an *aesthetic* of change.

Yet for all the interpretative potential that might be suggested by the patterning above, one could track Bacher's oeuvre and find different, equally troubling, indefinite, though seemingly personal repeated foci. Her affiliations to other artists, say. Beginning again with *3 Standard Stoppages* and Bacher's gender fucking, we can glimpse an ongoing conversation with mostly male creative figures, not dissimilar to (though less extreme and ventriloquized than) that performed by Sturtevant. Duchamp regularly, from Bacher's use of readymades to the broken mirror, *Big Glass* (2008), to the giant chessboard and sculpture work *Chess* (2012), with its bicycle wheel, to the rubber *Toilet* (2013); Dan Flavin and Jasper Johns in the pink fluorescent light *Pink out of a Corner (To Jasper Johns) 1963* (1991); and Warhol repeatedly—from the *a, A Novel*-like recordings and transcripts of *Do You Love Me?*, to works relating to Jackie Kennedy, to *Sleep* (1996), a real-time

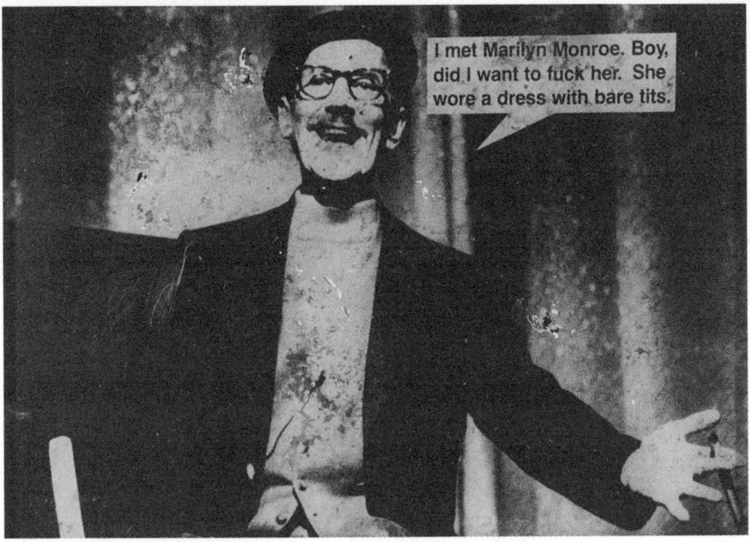

Lutz Bacher, *Jokes (Groucho)*, 1987

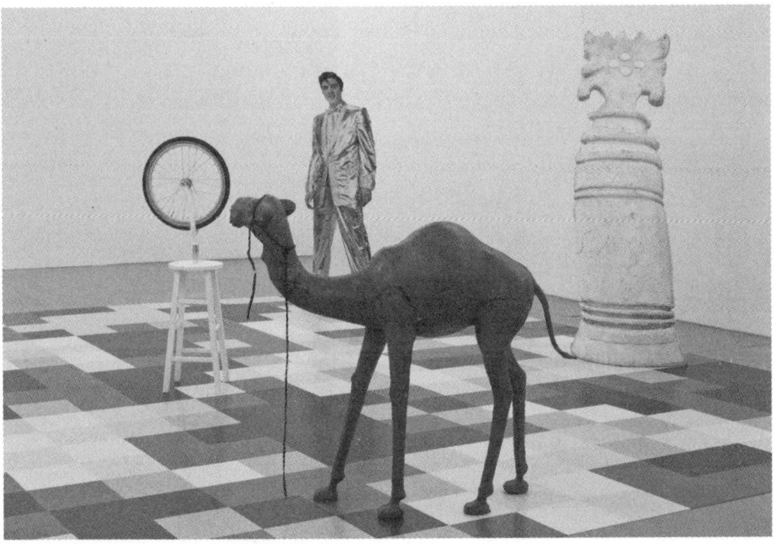

Lutz Bacher, installation view of *Chess*, 2012

performance and CCTV video of Bacher sleeping in the Gramercy Park Hotel, to her 2015 multichannel, red-white-and-blue-toned video of the Empire State Building (the Perspex projection screens held in place by sandbags, recalling Hurricane Sandy) and numerous others in between. There are references, in Bacher's titles, to Jorge Luis Borges, David Foster Wallace, Blinky Palermo, Jackson Pollock, *Spies Like Us*, Van Gogh, the Beatles, Dr. Seuss, Jimi Hendrix, *The Way We Were*, J. G. Ballard, Camper van Beethoven, George R. R. Martin ...

"Constellation," though an increasingly overtaxed term in art discourse, might be a catchall to employ here, not least since Bacher has worked with star arrays themselves. In 2011 she produced *The Celestial Handbook*, eighty-five framed pages of found empyrean—spiral galaxies, Alpha Centauri, nebulae, comets, star clusters—from amateur astronomer Robert Burnham Jr.'s 1966 book of the same title. One might read such work, succeeding as it does four decades of artworks that point, however obliquely, to the depredations of life on Earth, as a dream of escape (à la Stanley Brouwn's). But the heavenly photographs—imperfect transmissions, while fitting into Bacher's tendency toward glitch-laden, raw photography and film and object making—also convey themselves within another, open-ended stream of her work that revolves around the literally unearthly.

In 1996, through the window of her house in Berkeley, California (she's more recently moved to New York), Bacher filmed *Blue Moon*, a work that "ironically literalizes," as Caoimhín Mac Giolla Léith has written, "the precise meaning of a phrase most often deployed metaphorically—that is, a second full moon appearing in the same calendar month—in that the refraction of the moon's image through the window pane and/or camera lens produced a second moon, which was smaller but clearer, on account of the optics involved."[7] In her 2013 exhibition at Portikus, in Frankfurt, Bacher embedded video monitors showing this work in a lunar desert of black coal slag. By the time it traveled to the ICA in London, the black desert, *Black Beauty* (2012), supported *Ashtray* (2013), a plangent and vaguely humanistic metallic object, like a handmade rover (albeit one containing an ashtray), while around the space drifted an audio work, *Puck* (2012), of a man with Down syndrome repeatedly essaying lines from *A Midsummer Night's Dream*: "If we shadows have offended, / think but this, and all is mended." At the ICA, soundtracking the aforementioned *Chess*—which includes a cutout of Elvis Presley, the type one might find in an old-fashioned movie theater—Bacher set up *Elvis* (2009), a loop of Presley singing the wordless falsetto outro of *Blue Moon* (1956). Here, he's a man who sounds like a woman, his voice merging with echoes of Duchamp. Everything interfuses, alloys, slips.

❀

One broad stylistic approach nevertheless undergirds all the misfit trajectories and asterisms of Bacher's art, liaising with its prolixity. She favors low-grade, borrowed broadcasts, second- and third-generation reproductions that accrete substantial blemishes, mixing signal and noise. The noise speaks as well as the signal—"one big ruin," as Bacher describes her work in one interview[8]—and slows the viewer as, say, an old, hissy bootleg does. You strain to hear what's there; the listening is active. You might indeed be "hearing things" that say as much about you as they do about the artist, just as the questions Bacher's interviewers pose in *Do You Love Me?* are inadvertent confessionals. The noise transmits in another way too. It says Bacher is an artist who needs simultaneously to speak and not speak—needs to do so through others, to smokescreen what she says. Hobbled communication is still communication. It's the largest double, or binary, in a gestalt of doubles that ranges from reapplied media images to double moons to black deserts and white ones, collapsing presence and absence into each other.

This arrangement must be reactive, lest it calcify. Bacher's art is given life by her life's unpredictability—for example, *Huge Uterus* (1989), a video recording her operation for fibroid tumors—and appears, at the time of writing, to have responded to her rising profile in the art world by flinging out bedlam by the fistful; the very *procedure* of making—overproducing—now becomes important. By the final pages of *SNOW*, Bacher seems to be creating constantly, without interrelation. The works are dated by day. On March 23, 2013, alone she thinks up *Ft. Lauderdale*, "a diving boardlike structure out of aquamarine plastic panels," *The Thinker*, a Rodinesque "sitting female mannequin," and *Cannibal Love Song*, a red circle of folded and unfolded vinyl. As the outpouring keeps going, through sculpture, performance, photography, video, it feels like one holistic, gnarly thing. Her sprawling website (www.lutzbacher.com), meanwhile, is as immersive as any actual net artist's. Not surprising for a figure who effectively predicts our collective vanishing behind avatars.

These recent pursuits, though consistently raw and anxious, admittedly don't necessarily always flaunt Bacher's semi-signature technical degradations on the plane of their individual aesthetics. Rather, in concert they allow flooding itself to become distortion. In so doing, they still point to messy signaling and how that messiness can be—to echo a title she uses regularly—a "gift." Objects and images, when roughed up, are enlarged, made galactic; they gain something by becoming, in digital media's parlance, "lossy." An artist's public image is like that too. Subtracting information, Bacher has enlarged herself, pragmatically. Recognizing the cult of personality that clings to artists, she's made herself a personality in absentia, à la Warhol and Duchamp, a character not reified but accepting that people are more spacious than any image put on them. There is a philosophy, too, of reception at work here. Recognizing up front that viewers never get a full picture, always inject partialities into whatever they see, Bacher doesn't even try to present one; what she offers instead is explicitly speckled with holes and gaps to populate. She fashions something that fosters public fascination—call it mystique—and that serves as a shield, telescopes her most overt concerns. There is violence everywhere, her work implies, as it brutalizes images and objects and reveals brutality's operations in the world, and it is a small violation within the larger ones, a disarming, to become the object of knowledge. So do I love her? I don't even know her. But yes, I do.

1. See Lutz Bacher, *Do You Love Me?* (New York: Primary Information, 2012).
2. Lutz Bacher, *SNOW*, ed. Gregor Muir, Sophie von Olfers, and Beatrix Ruf (Zurich: JRP|Ringier, 2013), unpaginated.
3. Virginia Woolf, *Orlando: A Biography* (Orlando, FL: Harcourt, 2006), 226.
4. Bacher, *SNOW*, unpaginated.
5. Liz Kotz, "Sex with Strangers," *Artforum*, September 1992, 84.
6. Bacher, *SNOW*, unpaginated.
7. Caoimhín Mac Giolla Léith, "Peculiar Galaxies," *frieze*, October 2013, http://www.frieze.com/issue/article/peculiar-galaxies/.
8. Bacher, *Do You Love Me?*, unpaginated.

Forever Incomplete

He didn't leave much behind, and he didn't intend to. Christopher D'Arcangelo's brief burst of artistic maturity—four years from 1975 onward, a handful of exhibitions and a few institutional actions—bequeathed no legacy of objects, only Super 8 documentation of one-off events and some paperwork, memories, rumors. No critical writing on him circulated during his lifetime. Until 2011 there was no art-historical consciousness of his work, no retrospective exhibiting of archival materials. And there is no D'Arcangelo himself. In 1979, at the age of twenty-four, in what some have interpreted as the deliberate finale in a trajectory of artistic dematerialization, the artist hanged himself. Art history forgot him, and when it tried to grasp him again, its hands pretty much passed through.

To reach D'Arcangelo's sunless endpoint and the potential rationales behind it necessitates tracking back and infilling a number of overlapping contexts. Born in 1955, the son of notable Pop artist Allan D'Arcangelo, he was dyslexic, didn't finish high school, and didn't go to art school. Still, by 1974, in his teens, D'Arcangelo had been hired as a technician and general sweeper-up at the respected John Weber Gallery in Manhattan's SoHo, which collaborated with and operated as an afternoon hangout for a coterie of steely intellects: Minimalist, Post-Minimalist, and Conceptual artists including Carl Andre, Robert Smithson, Daniel Buren (whom D'Arcangelo would assist), and Ian Wilson. At this time he was already making precocious work, creating "paintings"—almost all since destroyed—involving empty squares fashioned from angle irons, their frontages painted, placed on shelves or on the wall. In moving forward from these—voids that anticipated later voids—a rapport with one of the older artists was particularly important. Wilson, some time earlier, had outlined a circle on the floor and then declared he would make no more physical artworks, only designate conversations as art. D'Arcangelo, who would play chess with Wilson and listen to his advice, from a ramshackle chair in his apartment, that the younger artist read Plato's gnomic dialogue *Parmenides*—which argues that if things are the case, they must also logically not be the case—soon came around to the idea of abandoning physical artistic artifacts himself.

At this point, one might also want to factor in the mid-1970s zeitgeist: the vestigial countercultural revolution, Vietnam War protests, a holdover belief in the revolutionary creation of a new society—which some artists at the time believed they might spearhead—and the evolving cultural favoring of going "blank." (Richard Hell and the Voidoids' album *Blank Generation* came out in 1977, the midpoint of D'Arcangelo's institutional intercessions.) The mainstream art world was seen very much as part of the toxic administering system, conflated with it. And as the '60s soured, this political position met another contemporaneous headwind, the dematerialization of art. It led to outfits like Jon Hendricks, Poppy Johnson, and Jean Toche's Guerrilla Art Action Group, who in 1969—themselves to some degree influenced by Viennese Actionism—set four people fighting in the lobby of MoMA until they were covered in the animal blood concealed in their clothing, a protest against MoMA board members, the Rockefeller family, whitewashing its involvement in weapons manufacture for Vietnam via art. It led, too, to Tony Shafrazi's notorious 1974 graffitiing of Picasso's *Guernica* with the mixed-up phrase "Kill Lies All"[1]—the future gallerist's statement against the release of a US officer responsible for the My Lai massacre in Vietnam. Guerrilla actions in general were a hot notion, while the impetus behind heists on social space had slid from flowery idealism to punkish nihilism. D'Arcangelo, shifting the emphasis in a way that jibed with the problem of commoditization that the artwork made blazingly evident, would go to bat for anarchism, a social system that had not yet been tried and one that also served to remonstrate—by not being graspable as a system—against the ones that had. All of this set the agenda, as he turned twenty, for direct actions in mainstays of the art establishment.

❀

Between 1975 and 1978 D'Arcangelo planned and carried out six ephemeral events, each differently weighted and context-specific, five of them filmed by his girlfriend, Cathy Weiner. On January 31, 1975, at the Whitney Museum, midway through the biennial, he chained his wrists to the front door at the end

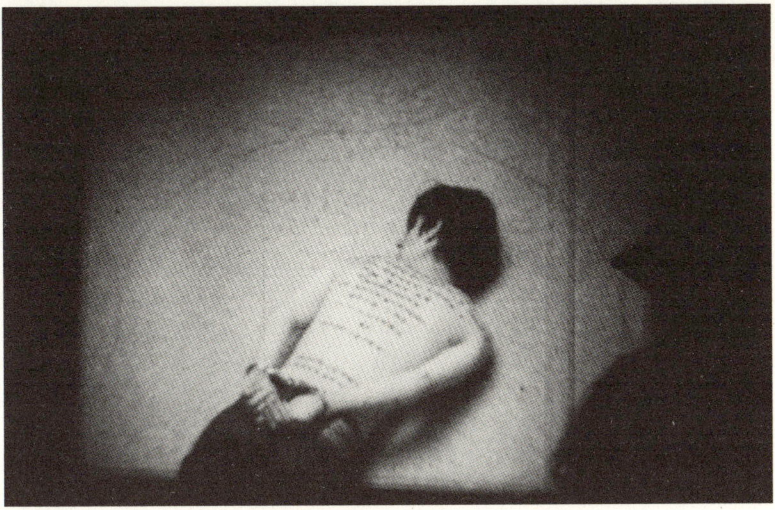

Christopher D'Arcangelo's action at the Solomon R. Guggenheim Museum, New York, May 3, 1975

of the Marcel Breuer building's short drawbridge, causing museum visitors to pile up and bottleneck on the bridge and behind the doors. He was shirtless in thirty-degree heat, and stenciled on his back was the legend that would become an accompanying credo for all his interventions: WHEN I STATE THAT I AM AN ANARCHIST, I MUST ALSO STATE THAT I AM NOT AN ANARCHIST, TO BE IN KEEPING WITH THE (_ _ _ _) IDEA OF LONG LIVE ANARCHISM / ANARCHISM. (The final four words were, as here, printed upside down.) When D'Arcangelo went to work, security was flummoxed. After fifteen to twenty minutes, there was a response on the institution's part: first a maintenance man arrived with a pair of three-foot-long wire clippers, which D'Arcangelo said would not cut the case-hardened padlock and chain; then, half an hour later, a folding screen was positioned between D'Arcangelo and the crowd, literally screening off the unsanctioned "artwork." Behind it, the artist pulled out his own key, unchained himself, and walked away.

The next month, at MoMA, on the anniversary of Shafrazi's attack on *Guernica*, D'Arcangelo spray-painted a gift-shop print of the painting with the phrase, "Kill Lies All," took it to the room where the painting was, and stapled it to the wall. He was about to spray a stencil of his with the statement, "When I state that I am an anarchist ..." on top when he was grabbed by a security guard, interrogated by museum staff in a restroom, and arrested. He refused to let his father pull strings to have the charges dropped, and later agreed not to do anything similar in MoMA again in return for a conditional withdrawal of the charges. In May, at the Solomon R. Guggenheim Museum—the year before, at the John Weber Gallery, Hans Haacke had mounted a show listing the affiliations of this institution's board members—D'Arcangelo undertook a different though again focused action. He lay down on the floor of the rotunda, the anarchist declaration again flowing neatly down his back, his arms and legs handcuffed behind him, the keys this time in a little envelope on the floor a short distance away. A Guggenheim employee alerted the police, who roughly dragged him up, tried to hustle him out, and after it was clear that he couldn't walk, freed D'Arcangelo via the keys (whose presence a bystander pointed out), and told him to go home.

In late July, D'Arcangelo went to the Metropolitan Museum, toting a stack of flyers bearing the following proposal:

> The Open Museum Proposal
> To The Metropolitan Museum of Art,
>
> The museum functions as a "criteria space," it determines the value of objects and activities in our daily lives. By supporting certain objects the museum creates an unbalanced system of values in the world. In order to determine the relationship of the needs of our daily lives and the values put forth by the museum I am making the following proposal;
>
> A. That The Metropolitan Museum of Art open its doors for seven consecutive days to any one wishing to place any object or perform any activity in the museum.
>
> B. That the museum vanquish its power to control that nature of the above objects and activities.

C. That all works of art now installed by the museum not be removed for the seven days.

D. That the museum purchase television and radio time to invite people to take part in this seven day event.

In conjunction with this proposal I am now performing a work which is being done in the spirit of the open museum.

In the museum's Great Hall, he removed his shirt, chained his ankle to a bench, and placed the flyers beside him. The guards' response, in this case, was less patient than on previous occasions.

At the Norton Simon Museum in California in 1976, D'Arcangelo spray-painted his customary statement onto the reflective plastic sheeting protecting a painting from weathering before, according to a later account in *Artforum*, "being tackled by a guard and carted off by the police."[2] In March 1978, at the Louvre, D'Arcangelo went a step further. He lifted Thomas Gainsborough's *Conversation in a Park* (1745)—a "conversation piece" long predating Wilson's conversation pieces, but their inverse in terms of materialist commodity status—off the wall, propped it up, and in the empty space pinned up an authority-querying, xeroxed statement: WHEN YOU LOOK AT A PAINTING, WHERE DO YOU LOOK AT THAT PAINTING? WHAT IS THE DIFFERENCE BETWEEN A PAINTING ON THE WALL AND A PAINTING ON THE FLOOR? (Another, related question: What was the relative status of Gainsborough's artwork and D'Arcangelo's?) This time, anyway, he got away.

From here on in, the removal would focus on D'Arcangelo himself: he would foreground the spaces in which he worked rather than the traditional saleable art objects that might have populated them, establishing his presence through a kind of absence. A highly capable carpenter and laborer, D'Arcangelo, in 1977, would begin undertaking building jobs with fellow artist Peter Nadin, situating them—via flyers that detailed the labor involved, materials used, and time spent, and invited others to view the "functional constructions"—in a speculative threshold zone between labor and art, between the makers' means of subsistence and their professional practice, questioning the division between the two. Invited to contribute to a 1978

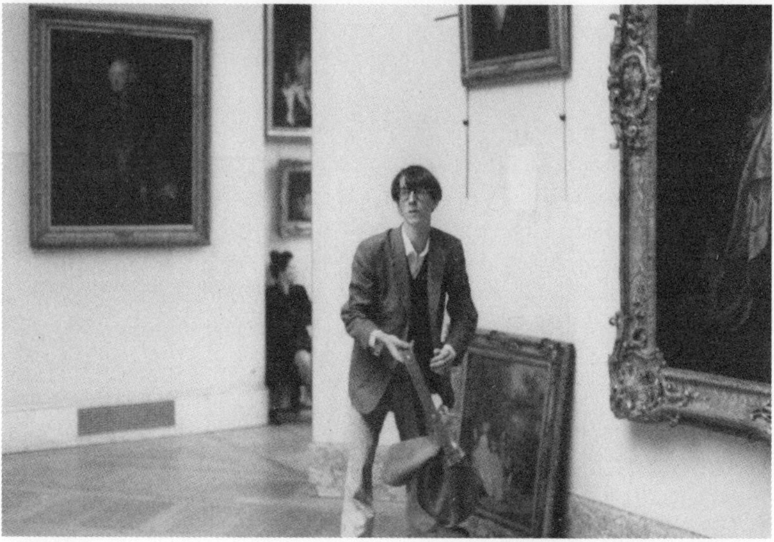

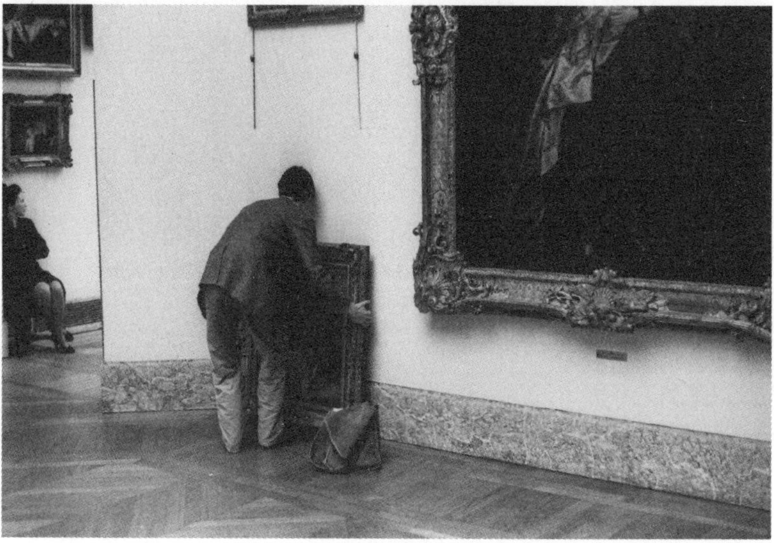

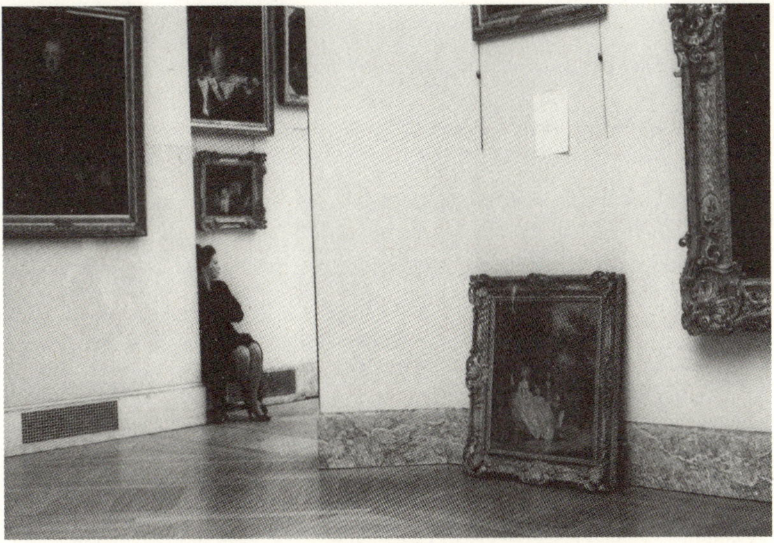

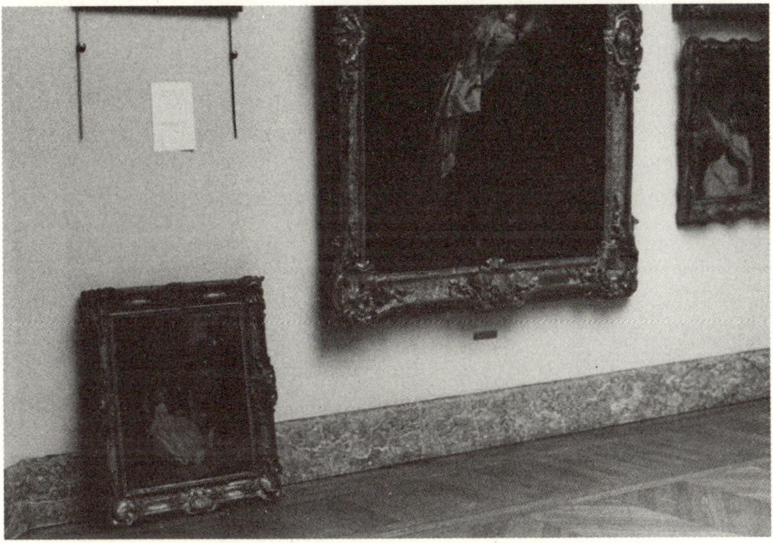

Christopher D'Arcangelo's action
at the Louvre Museum, Paris, March 8, 1978

group show at New York's Rosa Esman Gallery, D'Arcangelo asked for a written invitation—apparently customarily, this being part of the work—before requesting that his space be given to any citizen who wanted to use it.[3] When this was nixed, "he arrived, unauthorized, at the opening to sell apples at the entrance."[4] The same year, for a show at Artists Space, he insisted his name be left off all publicity materials, replaced by a blank space. His exhibition contribution, meanwhile, was *Four Texts for Artists Space*, a description and critique of the venue as an "independent" gallery. He wrote, in part:

> It is implied in the brochure that Artists Space shows work that is not shown in galleries and museums. Perhaps this is so. But the support for Artists Space is, in an indirect way, the same as the support for galleries and museums. Artists Space receives its main support from tax dollars; galleries and museums from private money. The government invests our money to maintain itself and, at the same time, to maintain the full social, cultural, and economic system (capitalism). [...] Once it is understood that the support of Artists Space and the support of galleries and museums are one and the same, that the systems are one system, a discourse for change may be opened that will lead to tangible results, i.e., unqualified space and/or revolution.[5]

If a self-administered space was thus the only one left, a couple of months later D'Arcangelo accordingly put together an evolving, eight-month-long group exhibition at 84 West Broadway, starting with a presentation of the empty gallery—a "work" entitled *30 Days Work*, referring to the span of time that he, Nadin (who ran the space), and Nick Lawson (the artist who lived there) had spent turning the venue into a gallery prior to the show—and with other artists, including Buren, Sean Scully, Jane Reynolds, and Rhys Chatham, adding work (or, in the latter's case, a performance) to the exhibit. After D'Arcangelo's death, another work was added: Dan Graham, Louise Lawler, Nadin, and Lawrence Weiner stenciled their names onto the floor.

The year before, D'Arcangelo's intervention in the Los Angeles Institute of Contemporary Art's journal had been a blank spread. He wrote a prefatory note, stating that the pages belonged to the reader, who could remove them, do what they wanted with them, and "install the page anyplace in the viewing space of LAICA, at any time and in anyway [*sic*] you want"[6]—another handing back of agency to decision-makers outside the art industry. This, he wrote, was a transfer of control from the institution to the viewer, even as it nevertheless represented a form of "curatorial control." Such thoughts no doubt would have been factored into D'Arcangelo's proposal for the Van Abbemuseum in Eindhoven, unfinished at his death, in which he asked that the spaces be left empty and the public bring in whatever they wanted to exhibit. D'Arcangelo, needless to say, was hyperconscious of where control lives, even where it appears in the guise of freedom.

Until very recently, his entire bibliography was also a blank page. He had been a pioneer of what Andrea Fraser would later call institutional critique, but hardly anyone knew it. Jeffrey Deitch, after befriending the artist at John Weber (where the future curator, then a recent graduate, had finagled a job at the front desk), wanted to write a text about his work for the magazine *Art-Rite*, but when D'Arcangelo showed it to Carl Andre, the older artist told him to spike it. This twist would fold into the retrospective design of D'Arcangelo's art, his phantasmal non-presence within art history. Indeed, part of the difficulty of assessing him in retrospect is that *everything* aligns itself with a speculative design, including his death, and yet everything is also holed, left open.

However quixotic it might appear from this distance, D'Arcangelo had evidently pledged to live entirely for art: to put himself in harm's way in life, to test limits, to use his body in an oppositional manner. But his work lives beyond him in a strange fashion. It's resistant to positioning within art history in part because of its propositional reversing, which stems from anarchism: whatever D'Arcangelo seemed to state, he also wanted—à la Plato's non-oppositional dialogue—to state its inverse so that his art might not be possessed and, again, controlled from without. Making meets unmaking, articulation meets disarticulation. His art has accrued ironies in his wake: the artist who in 1978 graced the "capitalist" Artists Space with a non-purchasable artwork that critiqued the venue ended up, thirty-three years later, being honored by a retrospective there, a week before the occupation of Zuccotti Park by Occupy protesters—presumably, the exhibition was strategically timed. Even paradoxes, though, can be claimed for D'Arcangelo's art, such that it starts to take on eerie dimensions of anticipation in hindsight. "It is not the paradox but the space between the two parts of the paradox," reads a quote in one of his notebooks, dated 1975.[7]

❀

Four years later, on April 28, 1979, D'Arcangelo's suicide would create another unresolved space, period as ellipsis. Christopher D'Arcangelo died and was almost entirely forgotten, save the odd commemorative work like Christopher Williams's installation *Bouquet for Bas Jan Ader and Christopher D'Arcangelo* (1991). Following the 2009 donation of his writings, recordings, and film documentation of his actions to New York University's Fales Library & Special Collections, however—they had been kept by his father until the latter's own death in 1998, and were now made available for perusal[8]—he was restored somewhat, thanks to the enthusiasm of graduate students and curators and, to a degree, the consonance of his actions with the Occupy movement. There are waiting swamps in this, too: D'Arcangelo's own textual silence around his suicide and reasons thereof, and the muddiness of his motives—a controlling system and, arguably, the father figure conflate highly uneasily. And if he wanted to be fully, irreversibly vanished, it is notable that he did not destroy his archive. He might have anticipated, also, that the work would sustain itself to some degree in folklore, while its edges fuzzed into obscurity over time. How, his art asked and answered, do you add something that is also a subtraction, construct the irreducible, disappear and don't? Under the circumstances, the answer to that question remains—aptly—forever incomplete.

1. Apparently out of nervousness.
2. See Annie Ochmanek, "Forcible Remove," *Artforum*, January 2012, 91.
3. One suspects Maurizio Cattelan knew about this, as he notoriously gave up his space in a biennial to advertisers. He also, when given his own Guggenheim show, positioned a figure facedown in the rotunda.
4. Ochmanek, "Forcible Remove," 92.
5. Christopher D'Arcangelo, "Four Texts for Artists Space," cited in *Anarchism without Adjectives: On the Work of Christopher D'Arcangelo* (New York: Artists Space, 2011), 8.
6. Christopher D'Arcangelo, "LAICA as an Alternative to Museums," *Journal of Los Angeles Institute of Contemporary Art* (January 1977).
7. D'Arcangelo, cited in Ochmanek, "Forcible Remove," 91.
8. Thanks to a donation by Cathy Weiner and the D'Arcangelo Family Partnership.

A Realer Real

Back in the summer of 1994, when I was researching an undergraduate thesis that would attempt to link Karen Kilimnik, Jack Pierson, Jean Baudrillard, and Friedrich Nietzsche—picture the mess—I first stumbled on Laurie Parsons's name. University library, November 1991 *Artforum*, Jack Bankowsky's article "Slackers." In a text that would catalyze a mini-movement, the magazine's future editor anatomizes a break on the part of several young American artists with the polished stylistics of US art in the '80s: an approach that "tunes out," sprawls on the couch, feels grounded, *real*. Parsons, the default focus of a text that also mentioned Kilimnik, Pierson, and Cady Noland, was then still enough of an unheralded quantity that Bankowsky could at one point misspell her name, and he appears to have mixed feelings about her work, which, he reports, comprises proposals like *Stuff* (1990), a "loose tangle of junk [...] which she culled from a closet in her mother's house." This, for the writer, "screams hippie": "When she talks about her work/life, her language is littered with icky humanist sentiment. [...] Parsons insists she wants to make art outside the gallery, outside the institution of art. It all sounds familiar, eerily familiar—a mix of archaic vanguard sentiment and countercultural utopianism. Yet the accumulation of stuff—nonequivalent ideologies, mutating beliefs, random pressures, and plain accident—is strangely moving. We bliss out on the web of intersecting yet incommensurate meanings; it's the gesture rather than the revelation of autobiographical detail that ultimately counts."[1]

What Parsons desires, Bankowsky continues, is "to set up the conditions for a *real* encounter—for an encounter with the Real." By 1994 she had followed through. Right when I was reading, Parsons was enlarging the gesture, tuning out for good. In the first of a couple of surprising echoes of Charlotte Posenenske's career, she was in the process of exiting the art world after butting heads over a public proposal in Germany—specifically a sculpture park in Nordhorn, Lower Saxony. Here Parsons had offered several unwelcome ideas, their rejection evidently causing some simmering misgivings to boil over.

She suggested bringing the moon to hang over the park (though she clarified her meaning: "I meant it with warm feelings. Bring the moon to hang over Nordhorn each night that you may, that it is visible. I meant a sincere level of poetry here"). She proposed "a fountain that goes straight up." And she suggested "that visitors to the park be told that she had camped there for an entire year." This didn't have to be true. "Is not 'deception,' subterfuge, also real?"[2] Encounters, then.

That year, according to her friend/collaborator Bob Nickas's invaluable timeline in a later issue of *Artforum*, Parsons ditched a career she'd been slowing, for various reasons, over the last five years. Somewhere during that span she'd done something with tangibly good results, and this was a place she would increasingly want to stay in. She'd gotten to know a man around her neighborhood in Hoboken, New Jersey, who, he told her, had lived in a tent in a nearby park for more than a decade. Parsons discovered that while he was eligible for subsidized housing, he wasn't mentally capable of going through the paperwork process to get it. Finding herself able to help, she undertook similar mediations and has now done so for many years: "interviewing children for a study on physical and mental health at a Newark hospital; taking part in an art program for adolescents with a history of psychiatric hospitalizations; most recently, working with the National Alliance for the Mentally Ill."[3]

Parsons doesn't mention to her coworkers that for seven or eight years in the '80s and early '90s she was an artist. She doesn't read articles about her former career. When a work of hers was lent to a group show at David Zwirner in 2010, she had to be coaxed into seeing it and was reportedly uncomfortable with looking back. But if she's somewhere else now, it took —at least partly—the maneuverings and shortfalls of the art world itself to bring her there, "outside the institution of art," into a realer real.

❀

Parsons first pops up, circa 1986/87, in a New York group show —she'd sent slides to the gallery and had been invited—wherein she exhibited things she'd found on roaming walks through the environs of New Jersey and brought back to her studio, where

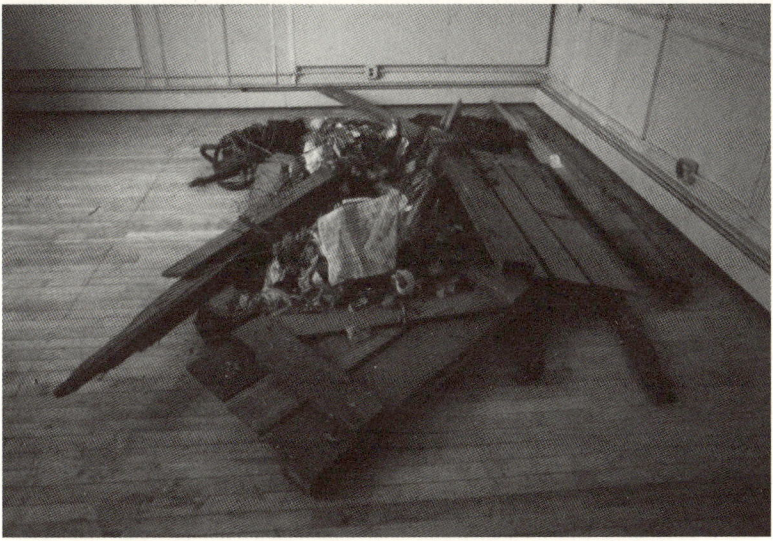

Laurie Parsons, *troubled*, 1989

they'd have to prove themselves over time. The ones that did so were the ones that, for her, had the gravitas of art, the accidentalness and verve of life. A blue-and-brownish-red-striped mattress, propped upright, with a single spring rip in it; a pair of gridded metal chairs, stacked, holding a boxy something wrapped in brown paper; stray pieces of wood. She followed this with a one-person show at Lorence-Monk Gallery, wherein she arranged objects found over the course of a year around the edge of the space in the order she'd found them: a Beck's beer bottle, a suitcase, a noose, a log, etc. She later recalled she had titled one piece—"an inverted triangle formed by three lengths of a bed frame with the two longer sides crossed at the bottom"—*V.*, after the 1963 Thomas Pynchon novel. The nature of V., in the book, is never clarified: more "intersecting yet incommensurate meanings," as Bankowsky had it;[4] more evidence of the complex, shifty life of things. Nothing sold. It would only be when things *did* sell that Parsons developed problems.

Before that happened, she would progress from individual items to landscape gestalts, covering the floor of one gallery with *Field of Rubble* (1988), which pulled its materials from a plateau near the Hudson River, a mixture of rubble and, Parsons told Nickas, "packets of soy sauce, keys, butts of lottery tickets."[5] The works assume the format of scatter installations. See three works from 1989: *Pieces*, a floor-bound offhand calligraphy of paint tin and lid, paint-stained paper, metal, and disinfectant bottle; *Dried Mud, Rocks, etc*, whose "etc" also appears to include a central metal rim and some crumpled paper; and *troubled*, which vaguely resembles one of Joseph Beuys's sleds, if his sleds were made out of a filthy mix of pallets and giant splinters, topped with swept-up dirt, newspapers, crumpled cans, and, most notably given the title, a woman's shoe, and accoutered with ominous black rope.

Troubled did sell: Nickas recalls being involved in the deal and this being one of merely a handful of works Parsons had sold up to that point. What appears to have thrown her, though, was the selling out of her entire show at the Cologne gallery of Rolf Ricke—a gallery that, fittingly, also showed Barry Le Va, whose own scatter installations from the mid-1960s onward provide a kind of formal template for Parsons's diffusions (as well as those of Kilimnik and Noland). Collector Alfred Greisinger bought the show, which contained all the works from Parsons's first solo—the log, the suitcase, the noose, etc.—on the sincere basis that the parts ought to be kept together. For Parsons, though, the idea that someone would pay (presumably handsomely, since she also sold a single discarded pink bathroom sink, flipped upside down and creature-like, for three thousand dollars)[6] for things she had collected on the street was wholly disorienting. The convertible value of her looking wasn't a factor for her, it seems, nor the time that the work had simmered in her studio, waiting to be defined as acceptable or not, nor the fact that her work clearly stood in a near eighty-year history of readymades and found objects validated as art. For Parsons, apparently, the work remained on the other side of the Rubicon, remained what it was on the street—a (literal) collection of complex discards, bristling with life and potential ambiguity, and the gallery was only a means to *see* it.

This was the end of her selling career—she told Lorence-Monk that nothing else was to be offered for sale—and pretty much the end of her working with objects. From this point there would be no commodities, and if money were to be involved, it would flow in the other direction. First, as the United States went into recession in 1990, Parsons "exhibited" an empty gallery (albeit with a fresh coat of paint) at Lorence-Monk; an invite was sent out without her name on it and the artist later removed the show from her CV, as if completing a negative cycle. The following year she was invited to show in an institution in Rottweil, southwestern Germany. Merging artistry with everyday life and basic decency, offering the best possible alternative to purchasable objects, she proposed (and was permitted) to move into the gallery for the show's seven-week span and also to work in a local psychiatric hospital; she also worked with developmentally challenged children.

At the start of 1992, for the group exhibition "The Big Nothing or Le Presque Rien" at New York's New Museum, she exhibited a stack of three hundred dollar bills and informed the guards that they mustn't stop people from taking the money. For another show at the same institution later the same year, "The Spatial Drive," the guards again came into play. Parsons, who was invited to create an educational framework for the exhibition, presented the first stage in a still-extant project in which, initially, all info texts were removed by the institution, information being offered instead by well-briefed guards—guards who, nevertheless, delivered their own slant, the work thus continuing the open-endedness that had been a hallmark of Parsons's work—and afterward by invigilators who were encouraged to meet the artists before the exhibition and learn about the works they were guarding, that they might tell visitors about them. This was, or rather is, Parsons's last work of art. She still makes notes, but she doesn't publish or share them. Her only acts now are, again, in the negative: in 2006, according to Alexander Koch, she convinced "a major German collector" (presumably Greisinger) not to loan a work of hers to the 4th Berlin Biennale. If she can help it, the work isn't seen.

❦

And so the arc is an outwardly straightforward one. The artist begins on the street, what she finds there becomes art, the art becomes material goods, and when she doesn't like that, she dematerializes and segues into quantifiable assistance. In some ways, even though Parsons was arguably the first artist to bring

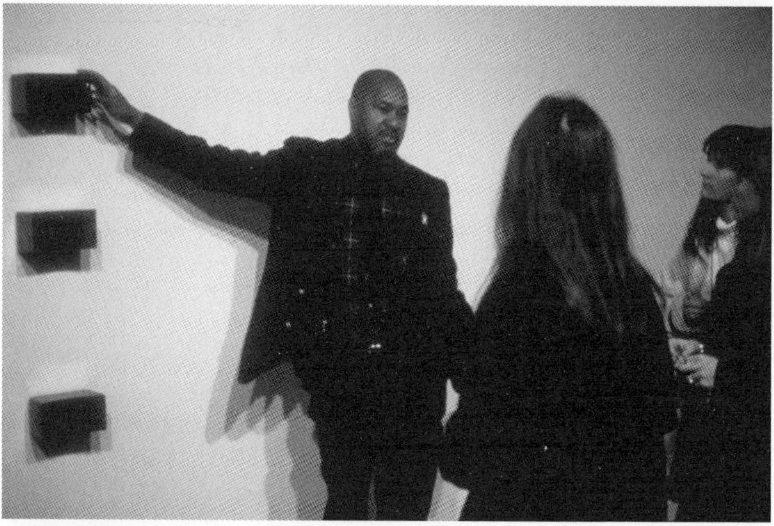

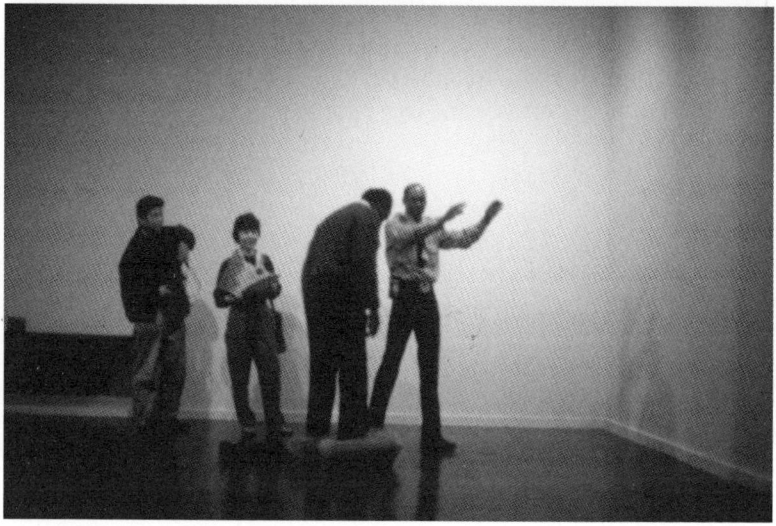

Laurie Parsons, "The Spatial Drive: Security and Admissions Project," exhibition view, New Museum, New York, 1992–93

total trash into the gallery, her story (and her art) is strongly retro—"eerily familiar," as Bankowsky had it—or at least a conflation of retrospective moments into something only semi-new, new only in degree. It partakes of the readymade and found object and all that these entail vis-à-vis meaning, value, and visuality; of Post-Minimalist scatter installation; of Conceptual art's propositional nature. (See, for instance, an earlier example of discards as art, Rafael Ferrer's 1968 *Three Leaf Pieces*, in which the artist placed sweepings of dead leaves in the elevator leading to the Dwan Gallery and in the Castelli Gallery itself and its stairwell; see also David Hammons's later work with urban-street detritus.) Parsons's art echoes Robert Smithson's non-sites and the general back and forth of art and environment prevalent in the late 1960s. It echoes the empty-space continuum from Yves Klein to Michael Asher to Christopher D'Arcangelo. Even Parsons's anxiety and disavowal is familiarly redux, a direct echo of Posenenske's, right down to the chosen ameliorative alternative, with occasional shades of Cady Noland's after-sales control.

This is not to fault her—nobody could gainsay Parsons's sincerity or her ethical life choice—only to say that her career capsules a predicament that, for a certain personality type, won't go away. We'll see it again. You try the art world. It tries you in return. Eventually you return to the real and you help; in the eyes of those you've left behind, the purity of intent you couldn't achieve before is now yours. And, you know, whatever.

1. Jack Bankowsky, "Slackers," *Artforum*, November 1991, 98–100.
2. Laurie Parsons, quoted in Bob Nickas, "Whatever Happened to: Laurie Parsons," *Artforum*, April 2003, 202–5.
3. Ibid.
4. Bankowsky, "Slackers," 98.
5. This work, kept in Parsons's storage unit, would later join the storied ranks of "art thrown away by workers who don't know that what they're throwing away is art."
6. This was the work shown at Zwirner in 2010.

Freedom's Just Another Word

Tucked away at the back of Bruce Hainley and John Waters's *Art: A Sex Book* (2003) is a nine-part questionnaire addressed to and answered by Cady Noland. By this point, the artist outwardly had plenty of time to make public statements, even if she virtually never deigned to. It had been two years since she had exhibited a new work—which, upon the show's closing, she had demanded be destroyed, its parts stowed in different bins around Manhattan—and seven since her last solo exhibition. At the time of writing, it is nineteen years since that show and there have been no sanctioned solo exhibitions since, despite overtures from, among others, the Museum of Modern Art.

Hainley and Waters asked Noland if there is sexual innuendo in the art world. "Yes," Noland wrote. "Artists get 'screwed' by their dealers [...] art work and artist also begin with 'virginity' but may have 'deflowerments' by art world professionals."[1] They asked her why New York museums are so sexist. Noland pointed out that the Whitney and MoMA each had a Lauder ("as in Estée Lauder, cats and kitties") on their boards, thus being associated with men's domineering images of women; that MoMA, among others, "has their own DISMAL history 'with' women"; and that "the last Whitney Biennial had 80 men and 30 women. HOW SICK IS THAT? ... I ASSURE YOU, IT'S ALL VERY MUCH ABOUT SEX." They asked her if another contemporary artist's work had ever shocked her. "Mayhem shocks me," wrote Noland. She wrote, elsewhere, about how her art had been censored by a gallerist fearful of offending collectors. Then she didn't speak to another interviewer for a decade or so.

Her documented exhibiting career, a forensic analysis of culturally specific mayhem, lasted thirteen years (1988–2001). It proved long enough. Long enough for art history and auction houses; long enough to feel, for many observers, gallingly short; long enough for Noland to construct a portrait of contemporary America via stuttering, disorderly looking, modular installations and stand-alone sculptural stratagems that refused easy "consumption." These works came primarily in a palette of silver, black, and red-white-and-blue, and used familiar materials as if crime-scene evidence, which in her hands they were. Some of Noland's chosen items were synonymous with constraint: public stocks, cordons, stanchions, barriers, weapons, handcuffs, helmets, chains. Others resonated with leisure and consumerism: barbecue stands, burger buns, shopping baskets, trolleys, ramparts of stacked beer cans. Others with freedom: American flags, whitewall tires, license plates. Others with entertainment: trashy newspaper reports on celebrities and scandal-wracked figures, from Jack Nicholson to Patty Hearst, often presented as cutouts of the type you'd find in old movie-theater lobbies.[2]

Outwardly, these aspects look like opposites activated as dialectics. Constraint is the inverse of freedom and leisure is a function of the latter, a supposedly inalienable right. Yet everything Noland uses, as one might note on a surface level from the steely continuity between barriers and chains and supermarket trolleys, turns out to be part of a totalizing, secretly controlling system, one lacking an outside. The vicarious thrill of tabloid journalism, reflected by her various manners of using wire reports on celebrities as shorthand for media voyeurism and distraction, is in Noland's cosmology another cordon, a weapon, an analgesic within a society of control. So is shopping per se. There are no safe places. The red, white, and blue is all over your Budweiser; your Budweiser, which you thought you voluntarily chose, was pushed at you as a pacifier.[3] Freedom, to edit the lyrics of an old song, is just another word.

What all of this adds up to, insinuates Noland's fusion of '60s Pop, '70s scatter art, well-founded '80s anxiety, and intermittent invoking of Abraham Lincoln, is the endpoint of a country that couldn't live up to the ideals upon which it was founded. (Or as Lane Relyea writing about her work in 1996 smartly puts it, "A country driven delirious by its own sense of mission [...] committed to a destiny that won't reveal itself.")[4] A country, as Noland perceived and poeticized it, resultantly flooded with angry and barely analyzed frustrations that its overseers must strategize to control and redirect, letting them out as what she has called "individual forms of venting"—one-on-one violence, gendered or racial; or the vicarious viewing of famous people's downfalls—lest those energies be directed into collective revolt, a destructive mirroring of the once-respectable violence that founded the United States.

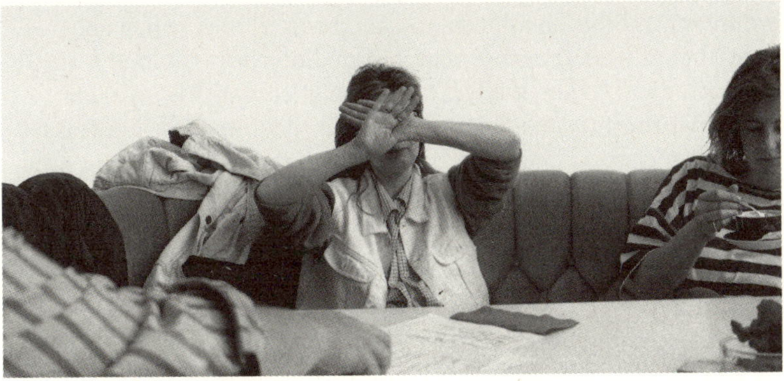

Cady Noland at documenta-Halle, 1992

One upshot of all this, Noland suggested in one of her extremely rare interviews, is that citizens learn to treat other people like objects.[5] And if this happens on the lowest rungs of society it also happens on the highest, incarnated in the kind of type-A personality that rules boardrooms and, notably, intersects with the latter-day art market either as a purchaser or a dealer. In 1987, for an academic conference in Atlanta on evil, Noland presented "Towards a Metalanguage of Evil," an essay powered by savvy distrust that analyzes society in terms of a secret game, a real reality behind the social facade, hints of whose rules glimmer in popular culture, in which strong, psychopathic personalities prey on and dominate the weaker. Paraphrasing Columbia University professor Ethel Spector Person, she wrote, "The psychopath shares the societal sanctioned characteristics of the entrepreneurial male."[6]

Noland, who based her aesthetics on treating *objects* like objects—pushing things without feelings brutally together—had her first solo exhibition in 1988, though reproductions are floating around of works from circa 1984 onward. She seems to have arrived fully formed but with expansions in waiting. By 1999, though, as artist Steven Parrino recalled, Noland was already in reverse: no longer showing solo, and making work that hid itself away—one of three new pieces she made that year for the Migros Museum in Zurich, Parrino wrote, secreted itself in a stairwell where virtually nobody would notice it.[7] Her last voluntary exhibition appears to have been in 2001, when she contributed work to a show curated by Bob Nickas, a long-term supporter and cogent analyst of her practice. On this occasion (again on Parrino's evidence), Noland used white plastic A-frames and painted wood planks as barriers and "nearly closed the room to viewers with [their] placement."[8] Since then, with one small, barely admissible exception—as we'll see—there has been no new work.

❁

Yet there has been activity. Is it ironic, or perfect, or perfectly ironic that Noland's own withdrawal has drawn her into the orbit of "entrepreneurial males" more than might otherwise have been the case, and that managing her post-career now takes up, to hear her tell it, all of her time? When Noland began pulling away from art in the mid-1990s, her decision was synchronous with the moment when the art world began ceasing to constitute an "outside" in itself, a place from which to speak truth to power (or what you will), and turned into something absorbed. First, some artists began aligning themselves with the type of sensationalist journalism Noland had positioned as instrumentalized, part of the so-called military-entertainment complex. (In barely consorting with the press throughout her showing career, Noland seems to have anticipated this, refusing to be celebritized insofar as she could.)[9] Then the galleries got bigger, the art world internationalized, biennial culture rose. For reasons well rehearsed elsewhere, contemporary art became ever more explicitly a luxury-goods market, a boutique for the superrich. This, too, was mirrored back at a vicarious public.

That is to say: Noland withdrew when the zone of critique itself blurred with entertainment and vanity sating. (Also in the year of 9/11, for what that's worth.) She withdrew while the objects of her prior study—socially acceptable and even widely admired exponents of self-interested behavior—were becoming themselves increasingly visible characters, chasing fresh apogees of status, in an art world that had become explicitly another field of business for, primarily, pushy and driven and manipulative men. Once again, it'd be possible—though Noland hasn't said she sees it this way—to see her actions since "quitting" as extramural yet borderline artistic, based less on identification of a problem (one component of her previous work) than on reacting to it (*another* component, rooted in her art's refusal of gratification). Turning, without making art—for reasons that will become clear—toward the workings of the art world itself, Noland has been tirelessly obstructive, wielding a sack of spanners amid the machinery, the sedulous executor of her own estate.

She quit solo shows at the age of forty, the point when, in recent decades, many artists' profiles have dipped because they're somewhat familiar, not the new kid on the block, exploring variation rather than innovation. The art world likes hot young artists and it likes reviving older ones after a few decades in the wilderness, but it doesn't, as a rule, favor artists between about the ages of forty and sixty. Noland, though, pointedly ceased production at the top of her game, which had the effect of ensuring a scarcity market for what she had already made. In 2011, her 1989 sculpture *Oozewald*, a cutout of Lee Harvey Oswald as he was shot, penetrated by holes where the bullets went, mouth plugged with an American flag, was auctioned for 6.6 million dollars, then the most expensive work by a living female artist. (Of course, Noland didn't see that money. Compare her disengagement from the market with Hammons's calculated playing of it, which is more akin to Hirst's.)[10] On occasion she has blocked auctions of her art.

In 2012 she was sued by Swiss dealer Marc Jancou when, on the basis that it was damaged, she disowned *Cowboys Milking* (1990), a cutout of a cow being forcibly milked, which he'd consigned to an auction at Sotheby's. Noland, a famously precise installer and user of space, closely attentive to the psychological charge of the objects she used, has said that many of her artworks in their current state are either damaged or missing parts. If this pains her, so does her work being placed in contexts she thinks inappropriate—primarily group exhibitions (since, again, she has refused all solo retrospectives) but also art fairs. In 2014 Noland refused to endorse her work's presence in a show in Connecticut by the collector Peter Brant, forbade photographers from filming her work even in the background, and insisted on a plaque being installed that clarified she didn't have the time or attention to present her art properly. (In 2012 she demanded that a gallerist include a similar disclaimer in his booth at Art Basel, which stated that Noland "does not consider Christopher D'Amelio to be an expert or authority on her artwork, did not select the artwork being displayed in this exhibition, and in no way endorses Mr D'Amelio's arrangement of her work.") Again in 2014, in the course of a lawsuit concerning the failed sale of her work *Log Cabin Blank with Screw Eyes and Café Door (Memorial to John Caldwell)* (1993), Noland made clear she did not approve this work as one of her own since it used replaced materials: "This is not an artwork," she stated. Her reaction to New York curatorial operation Triple Candie's mounting of a fake retrospective of her work in 2006—with careful and tabulated variations from the original, intended to undo any pretense of full mimicry—has not been recorded, but one would be surprised if it was wholly enthusiastic.

In a silence-breaking conversation with the writer Sarah Thornton for her 2014 book *33 Artists in 3 Acts*—Noland apparently accepts interlocution once every twelve or thirteen years—she said that tracking and reacting to situations in which her work is misrepresented now takes up all of her time, such that, to her regret, she can no longer create art anymore. On one occasion she made an exception, though this was seemingly—according to artist-blogger Greg Allen's research[11]—a strategic quid pro quo. In 2008, without fanfare, Noland seems to have exchanged a damaged work in the Walker Art Center Collection in Minneapolis for a new one, albeit a piece—an untitled shopping basket containing crash helmets and weaponry—that could have come from the late 1980s (see, for example, *Basket of Action*, 1988) but is dated 2008. Even in producing fresh artworks, Noland is not going to make anything really *new.* Or, to flip that position, there's no need to, since her critical position has not aged. America has not changed, only become more what she recognized it to be decades before.

Speaking to Thornton, the artist mentioned how much she had admired Hirst's direct sale of his work at auction, and she's presumably aware of the potential for interventions in art's infrastructure to be classed as art. If, riskily, one considers her gap-strafed "post-career" as an *extension*, in another field, of her prior practice—albeit one mostly composed of recalcitrant silence—then it is contiguous on several levels: not only, as we've seen, in that Noland has retained a focus on the psychopathic extremes of social behavior, but also in terms of iconography. (Psychopaths, she once said, act out principles latent in a culture.) Aside from cordons—and the art world is nothing if not a restricted-access space—what one chiefly sees, looking back over her work, is circular holes: the holes in her stocks, the holes that blast through faces and bodies silk-screened on aluminum, the hole in the center of her whitewall tire (hung as if lynched) in *Publyck Sculpture* (1993–94). Noland's father, the post-painterly abstract painter Kenneth Noland, famously made targets. Cady Noland made art as target practice in which the gun had already been fired. She made holes, and her career over the last two decades has been a hole—a "doughnut subject," whose missing center is the artist and her stated rationale for retiring. Plus, whatever we might call her focus on the art world itself today is already inherent in her earlier work, which situated the gallery as an institutional space that polices and controls meaning. (In at least one case, she placed barriers around a gallerist's desk.) Her art both reflected this supervision and played hell with it, hewing to deliberately incomplete if fearful scenarios. What Noland has done in the past two decades, meanwhile, comprises a blunt yet continually elaborated statement: if the game is corrupted, don't play, or at least don't let their standards become yours. That she was an outstanding artist while working within art's purlieus—prescient, forceful, poetic, brave—casts a lengthening shadow, particularly in an age where the edges of art practice are unprecedentedly blurry.

❀

The pure products of America go crazy (William Carlos Williams); a paranoid is someone in possession of all the facts (William S. Burroughs). Noland, in the scrupulousness of her refusal, might register as wild-eyed or well briefed. She took, and takes, extreme protective measures—track the progress, from her increasing secrecy toward the end of her active career, refusing to let anyone into her studio, to telling an interviewer her phone is tapped and recommending conspiracy books, to covering her face when a photographer's around. Her silence, of course, has boomeranged, only increasing attention toward her. Many are the writers and art-world insiders who have clasped Noland to their bosom, upraising her for doing what they, and most others, don't dare to: indict, to the point of almost complete withdrawal, that system whose dots she'd connected.

Thesis (and if this sounds like romanticizing, fine): for an artist operating on Noland's echelon of commitment, when the critical and the criticized collapsed together there may have been no other possible route but to walk away. Parrino points out that Noland's art was effectively a materializing of personal fears: the artist who made work about crashed cars was not just revisiting Warholian givens but was herself in a car crash at a young age, the artist who made work about plane crashes is afraid to fly, the artist who made work about Patty Hearst has a fear of cults. Noland, evidence suggests, was not *playing* with her subject matter but angrily terrified of it, and her anger and fear were channeled into articulacy. Deep entanglement led her all the way in and then out again. Not, it seems, all the way out (she's talked lately about a possible retrospective in a decade's time) but far enough. And thesis part two: artists don't *have* to have long careers. A starburst can be enough. That was Cady Noland, without a doubt, and they can't take that away from her.

1. Cady Noland, cited in John Waters and Bruce Hainley, *Art: A Sex Book* (New York: Thames & Hudson, 2003), 195.
2. Lutz Bacher, with whom Noland shares some artistic DNA, has used this form too.
3. See, for purposes of comparison, Bill Hicks's contemporaneous stand-up routines on the sedative powers of alcohol and television.
4. Lane Relyea, "Holy Crusade," *Parkett* 46 (1996): 73.
5. Cady Noland, interview by Michèle Cone, *Journal of Contemporary Art* 3, no. 2 (Fall–Winter 1990), http://www.jca-online.com/noland.html.
6. Cady Noland, *Towards a Metalanguage of Evil* (Ostfildern: Hatje Cantz, 1992), unpaginated.
7. See Steven Parrino, "Paranoia Americana: The New Work of Cady Noland," *Afterall* 11 (Spring/Summer 2005): 3–8.
8. This was the show in which Noland, "like a serial killer" (in Parrino's words), insisted the work be broken up and spread throughout bins.
9. Specifically, in the mid-1990s British artists starred in the papers for the first time—for their pseudo-bohemian antics, their relationships, their loudmouth quotes, their controversy-courting art. In some cases, this was straightforward fame chasing engaging the economy of attention; in others, such as that of Damien Hirst, the context of the art market and artistic fame would fold into the work.
10. See "Street Level," the chapter on David Hammons, pp. 61–71.
11. See Greg Allen, "Wait, What Cady Noland, 2008?," *greg.org: the making of* (blog), November 10, 2014, http://greg.org/archive/2014/11/10/wait_what_cady_noland_2008.html.

The Gift of Subtraction

Late in 2007, I went repeatedly to Tate Modern's exhibition "The World as a Stage," primarily to see one small black-and-white photograph—or, rather, a series of thirty-one such photographs presented one at a time and, as per the artist's instructions, rotated daily: Trisha Donnelly's *The Redwood and the Raven* (2004). The experience of this staggered, witchy display, which documents the headscarf-wearing dancer Frances Flannery performing, in front of a tree in a forest, a dance called *The Raven* choreographed to Edgar Allan Poe's 1845 poem, was borderline perverse. You couldn't grasp the moves, hear the poem, or precisely remember the previous images, so that the additive melded continually with the subtractive. (The raven in the poem famously answers queries with "nevermore.") You wanted more, aware that the more you received would equate to less. This, I already knew, was the American artist's conceptual wheelhouse. Earlier that year, in Manchester, at Hans Ulrich Obrist and Philippe Parreno's performance-art extravaganza "Il Tempo del Postino," I'd seen Donnelly deliver a drum-pounding, soprano-screaming, incantatory performance, *The Second Saint*, a fully confident yet, for all its noise, muted display, ending with the fall of four black obelisks, which resides in my memory as a roaring blank abstraction.

But then methodically parsing the actions, objects, and images proffered by the San Francisco–born Donnelly is not really the point. Thinking of them as interacting systemic units and conjectures about shaped reality, the fungible nature of space and time, and the strictures of art reception is more fruitful; as is considering them as disquisitions on how much—how much information, how much presence, how much conceptual connective tissue—an artist needs or ought to provide. And how subtracting can once again be a gift, can become content in the negative. Hers, then, is an art of timing and artfully mobilized viewer psychology—or at least that's where it starts. For her New York solo debut at Casey Kaplan in 2002, Donnelly rode into the opening on a white horse, dressed in Napoleonic garb, and, acting as ersatz courier, delivered the oration that the

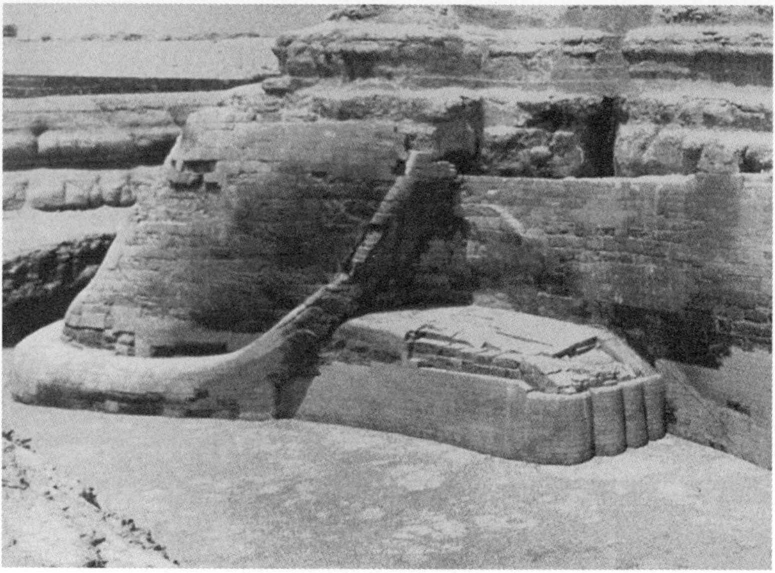

Trisha Donnelly, *Hand that holds the desert down*, 2002

French emperor supposedly should have given at the Battle of Waterloo: "If it need be termed surrender, then let it be so, for he has surrendered in word, not will. He has said, 'My fall will be great but it will be useful.' The emperor has fallen and he rests his weight upon your mind and mine and with this I am electric. I am electric." (Of this, eyewitness critic Jerry Saltz wrote, "At around seven o'clock on the night of April 5, 2002, Trisha Donnelly stole my esthetic heart," while reckoning that the performance rather outweighed the show itself.)[1]

By 2005 Donnelly didn't even require a real horse. Stage-managed rumor, mutable gossip as material was enough. At the opening of a show at the Kölnischer Kunstverein, celebrating a major artist's prize she'd won, word "got around" that another steed was waiting somewhere in the institution and that she would perform—artist-curator Beatrix Ruf remembers Donnelly left the preview dinner a few times to reinforce the idea. It never happened, but the very possibility colored the event. This, in microcosm, is what Suzanne Cotter has called Donnelly's ideal of the "uncontrived encounter," something the artist herself calls "natural use," and the carefully controlled outcome of so much of her work (which, in a gesture of imperial defeat that is also a gift, then abdicates control).[2] It's a process that, though the description may sound hyperbolic, comes closer to a suggestion of opening up space and time, with visibly disproportionate means, than almost any of Donnelly's contemporaries. See, for example, *Hand that holds the desert down* (2002), in which a black-and-white detail of one of the paws of the Great Sphinx of Giza flips into a mind-bending reframing of how gravity works, though a proposition whose method of disorientation—the choice of title—is blatantly evident.

Donnelly's art has prowled, avoiding resolution, around stormy transcendence from the outset. The first work of hers I remember seeing (and not being particularly struck by as her work has to accrete in the mind) was *Untitled (Jumping)* (1999), made before she graduated from Yale in 2000, in which she imitates a variety of musicians in states of musical rapture, while moving in and out of the video frame. Her art since, which encompasses sound works, actions, lectures, drawings, sculpture, photography, and more video, continually stresses the possibility of—to paraphrase the Bard—there being more in heaven and earth than is dreamed of in our philosophies. Or in our art world, which has a schizoid relationship nowadays to the esoteric and occult, liking it when historical—Hilma af Klint, say—but not so much when offered without irony or a sense that certain ancient fires haven't yet gone out. The thematic frameworks Donnelly sets up charge even her most outwardly slim works with electricity and expansive portent. The Napoleon slant, for example, continued in her sound work *The Vortex* (2003), which features a recording of the Slavyanka Russian Men's Chorus singing Mikhail Lermontov's poem "Borodino" (1837), named after a gruesome battle of the Napoleonic Wars. What this added was perhaps just another line of code, though it also aimed at an experience of synesthesia (see the anticipatory 2002 text "The Vortex Notes," which advised following the highest male voice and feeling it "compress like a photograph")[3] and dragged a vast historical event into the artwork's orbit, resituating it in the twenty-first century as a question that is particular and also diffuse. Her sculptures involving carving into quartzite, Donnelly has said, relate to "the enacting of processes of loss in geological time."[4] Entertain that, and millennia disintegrate as you gaze.

Or, rather, they might. Again, it's characteristic of Donnelly's art that one simultaneously falls under the spell and has a sense of how the spell is cast. What's likely is that no spell at all—or at best a pale shadow of a spell—is cast if this art is received secondhand, and here her work twists uncharacteristically polemical. In an age where so much art is experienced—if that's the word (sometimes it's just a pale afterglow)—through online aggregators and documentation, Donnelly's art insists on being taken in real time and real space, so that it can ask what those things even are. It's presumably to this end that she has given up doing interviews. A 2010 in-gallery conversation with Anthony Huberman at Casey Kaplan apparently most often featured the response "pass," with Donnelly playing tracks from her iPod in lieu of other answers—her catalogues don't usually feature essays and her press releases can veer strongly away from the interpretative. When a visitor attending her 2002 Kaplan show requested more info, he or she would be played some electronic beats. The PR handout for her poised, encrypted-feeling 2010 exhibition at Portikus, in Frankfurt, with its sequence of leaning incised-marble reliefs, drawings, and video, purports to be an explicatory text but is a list of titles and media.

This matters. One might wish it to be exemplary, except that it is turf that Donnelly almost owns and that, to mix metaphors, would become hackneyed fast. So much art today, as we're all aware, comes with an accompanying explanation that actively disarms the viewing experience, rationalizes it; and rationalizing appears to be the last thing Donnelly wants. Her art, in its myriad margin-directed speculations, says there's too much of that already, and not enough that, to paraphrase that horse-riding ensign, really rests its weight upon your mind and mine. Think for a second about how few artists actually sustain this quality of tactical, shape-changing surprise and risk. Meanwhile, galleries and fairs clog with frictionless production lines. Donnelly operates, conversely, a continual transitive process, new works adjusting old ones, the full picture held back. *Black Wave*, a 2002 photograph of a wave about to crest, feels—both in its minimal ominousness and its forceful incompletion—metonymic.

Donnelly stole this viewer's aesthetic heart a couple of times lately. Once was in Berlin at KW Institute for Contemporary Art's 2012–13 exhibition "One on One," in which viewers were permitted solo encounters with works of art. Commandeering a high floor, Donnelly presented a suspended sculpture, a big, steel-framed, partly cracked tray held up with airplane cables, like a perpetual enigmatic experiment. I remember low lighting, I remember the variable tilting of the oblique tray and water in it, but mostly I remember that characteristic quality of insistent wordless proposition: disbelief suspended, the author as artist erased and replaced, prospectively, with someone or something arcane and anxiety making, and then the figure of Donnelly, manipulating the murky theatrics, returning to mind.

Her tour de force of recent times, though, was a solo exhibition at the Serpentine Gallery in 2014. The exhibition was untitled; the works had no titles either. There was no official press release. There was, as ever with her, no core medium—"Donnelly genuinely has no medium," Hamza Walker once averred, accurately[5]—but the show gravitated toward video. It had been five years in the making, and had shifted terms several times over the half-decade.

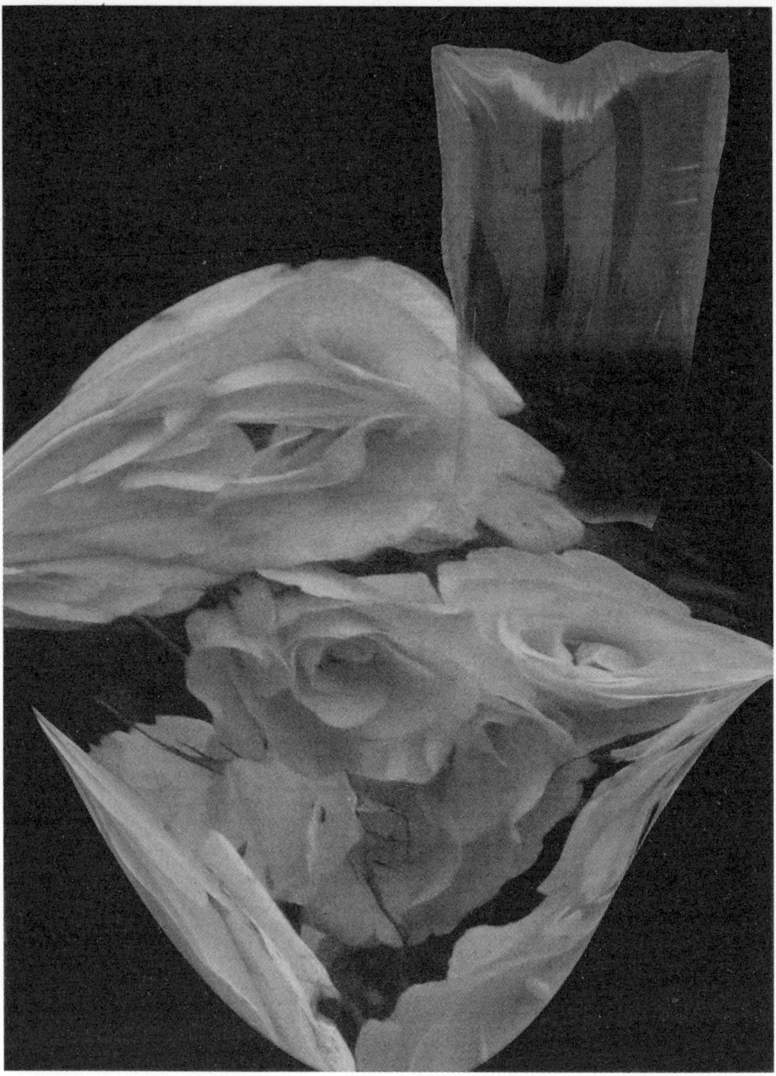

Trisha Donnelly, still from *Untitled*, 2014

As a conceptual anchor, she had returned to a liminal moment in the gallery's history—a series of renovations twenty years earlier, documented via photographs in the institution's archive, showing the metal studs beneath the cladding—and these had led her to remove sections of walls and open up another entrance to the gallery. What one received, whether filmic or still-based or sculptural, was gnomic: a weathered, truncated column that also resembled a loudspeaker, as if collapsing eons together; a video, at a skewed angle, of gilded, accelerated clouds; another of undulating liquid; a sound installation ranging from organ-like music to electronic chimes.

Albeit in abstract fashion, all this stagecraft positioned the work in *time*, made time an agent, left even standing stone open to the weathering caresses of light, as if capsuling time's touch. The website bore an apropos three-sentence codex from Donnelly: "I like late in the day. I like the day to night transfer, I like the desaturation. It's a high speed eternity."[6] Late light romances everything, unites it as a scene—scenery—and, as Donnelly implies, inveigles it into a simulation of history. Acceleration so that you can see things, or a proffered notion of the same. While the show was up, a rumor ran round the chattering classes—*another* rumor, keenly clasped—that you "had" to go during the magic hour, which the exhibition's late-autumn timing certainly sanctioned. So you went and the light dropped and revealed itself as the most sculptural—shaping—thing around. You moved amid hazy, thickened, falling, equivocal atmosphere, the architecture economically becoming star or, at least, gaining equal billing. You noticed the churchiness of the former teahouse's dome, myriad other architectural details both permanent and temporary. Yet while you flipped between what was definitely there, materiality, and a tumble of ghosting effects that transiently made the visible world more than it is, the feeling persisted—as with *The Redwood and the Raven*—that you weren't accessing a complete experience. The artist, while withdrawing, also appeared to withhold something as palpable as the dark side of the moon.

You knew she was orchestrating this; still, probably, you were seduced. This was, according to my asking around, many people's exhibition of the year—it turned up in several of *Artforum*'s annual best-of lists of 2014—yet few had anything articulate to say about it. And this, for someone who *had* seen it, was fine, was understood. "Perhaps evasion *is* her medium," Daniel Birnbaum wrote.[7] Donnelly skirts the public and, to some degree, the art world,[8] not incidentally to her practice—not because she's shy, antisocial, whatever; the few existing interviews, syntheses of confidence and musical voice, suggest otherwise—but centrally to its fluctuant reception. She also, these days, connectedly evades, sidesteps, feints past the snares of language, her own and others, underlining in the process how much of her work suggests memoranda issuing out of the distant or recent past, their lucidity eroded yet their allure redoubled by time's passage. The results discourse, so to speak, on verbalization's limiting force. To return to where these essays began, with Agnes Martin, just because you *can* funnel something through speech acts doesn't mean you're obliged to. There are registers of experience other and perhaps grander if more oblique and knotty than that, even if uncongenial to our post-Conceptual art world. Before the Serpentine exhibition opened I asked the institution if, on behalf of an art magazine, I might speak to Donnelly. Even before receiving a response, though, I'd grasped that I didn't actually want to quiz her, that the best possible outcome, given how her work requires not only our being there but its architect being gone, was that eventually relayed: Tell them I said no.

1. Jerry Saltz, "Thinking outside the Box," *Village Voice*, October 26, 2004, http://www.villagevoice.com/arts/thinking-outside-the-box-7138833.
2. Suzanne Cotter, "M. O.," in *The Hugo Boss Prize 2012* (New York: Guggenheim Museum, 2012), 14.
3. Trisha Donnelly, "In the Recombination of the Not So Vast Distance (The Vortex)," *Parkett* 77 (2006): 94.
4. Cotter, "M. O.," 14.
5. Hamza Walker, "As Free as the Squirrels," press text to accompany Donnelly's exhibition at the Renaissance Society, University of Chicago, 2008, http://www.renaissancesociety.org/publishing/32/as-free-as-the-squirrels/.
6. Trisha Donnelly, cited on the Serpentine Gallery website, see http://www.serpentinegalleries.org/exhibitions-events/trisha-donnelly.
7. Daniel Birnbaum, "Best of 2014," *Artforum*, December 2014, 264.
8. A curator friend of mine assessed her typical response time to an e-mail as "about four months," adding that the reply, when it came, would nevertheless be charming.

Biography

Martin Herbert is a writer and critic living in Berlin. He is associate editor of *ArtReview* and writes for international art journals. Previous books include *The Uncertainty Principle* (2014) and *Mark Wallinger* (2011).

Bibliographic Note

"Introduction" was published, in slightly different form, as "Maximum Withdrawal" in *Mousse* 47 (February 2015).

"Here and Not Here" was published, in slightly different form, in *ArtReview* 67, no. 5 (Summer 2015).

"The Gift of Subtraction" was published, in slightly different form, in *ArtReview* 66, no. 7 (October 2014).

Image Credits

p. 21 Agnes Martin, *Tremolo*, 1962. Ink on paper, 25.5 × 28 cm. The Riklis Collection of McCrory Corporation. Digital image © 2016 Museum of Modern Art, New York / Scala, Florence / VG Bild-Kunst, Bonn 2016.

p. 23 Agnes Martin in her studio in New Mexico, 1953. Photo: Mildred Tolbert. Courtesy of Harwood Museum of Art and Anna Bush Crews.

p. 32 Albert York, *Twin Trees*, ca. 1963. Oil on canvas mounted on masonite, 10 7/8 × 10 1/2 in. Private collection. Courtesy of Davis & Langdale Company, New York.

p. 35 Albert York, *Reclining Female Nude with Cat*, 1978. Oil on wood, 9 3/8 × 12 1/2 in. Private collection. Courtesy of Davis & Langdale Company, New York.

p. 43 Handlers rearranging Charlotte Posenenske's *Vierkantrohre Serie DW* (*Square Tubes Series DW*), Galerie Dorothea Loehr, Frankfurt am Main, September 9, 1967. © The Estate of Charlotte Posenenske. Courtesy of Mehdi Chouakri, Berlin; and Peter Freeman, Inc., New York.

p. 46 (above) Charlotte Posenenske, *Series D Vierkantrohre* (*Square Tubes Series D*), 1967. Configured by Rirkrit Tiravanija, 2010. Photo: Daniel Pérez. © The Estate of Charlotte Posenenske. Courtesy of Mehdi Chouakri, Berlin; Peter Freeman, Inc., New York; and Artists Space, New York.

p. 46 (below) Charlotte Posenenske, *Series D Vierkantrohre* (*Squares Tube Series D*), 1967. Configured by Ei Arakawa, 2010. Photo: Daniel Pérez. © The Estate of Charlotte Posenenske. Courtesy of Mehdi Chouakri, Berlin; Peter Freeman, Inc., New York; and Artists Space, New York.

p. 50 Stanley Brouwn, *This Way Brouwn*, 1960. Felt-tip pen and stamped ink on two pieces of paper, 24.5 × 32 cm. Courtesy of the artist and Konrad Fischer Galerie.

p. 57 Stanley Brouwn, *in diesem moment gehen x personen auf dem alexanderplatz in berlin in richtung norden. in diesem moment gehen x personen auf dem alexanderplatz in berlin in richtung süden*, 2012. Aluminum, matt black lacquer, 126 × 1 × 0.2 cm. Courtesy of the artist and Konrad Fischer Galerie.

p. 66 David Hammons, *Higher Goals*, 1986. Mixed media. (Five units) 35 × 30 × 30 in., 20 in. high. April 10, 1986–March 27, 1987. Photo: Pinkney Herbert / Jennifer Secor. Courtesy of Public Art Fund, New York.

p. 75 Lutz Bacher, *James Dean*, 1986. Still from video slide show, sixteen paired slides shown on two monitors, dimensions variable. Courtesy of Galerie Buchholz, Berlin / Cologne / New York.

p. 77 (above) Lutz Bacher, *Jokes (Groucho)*, 1987. Distressed photograph on aluminium, 97 × 150 cm. Courtesy of Galerie Buchholz, Berlin / Cologne / New York.

p. 77 (below) Lutz Bacher, *Chess*, 2012. Installation view at Portikus, Frankfurt am Main, February 9–April 14, 2013. Photo: Helena Schlichting. Courtesy of Portikus.

p. 85 Film documentation of Christopher D'Arcangelo's action at the Solomon R. Guggenheim Museum, New York, May 3, 1975. Photo: © Cathy Weiner. Christopher D'Arcangelo Papers; MSS 264. Courtesy of the Fales Library & Special Collections, New York University Libraries.

pp. 88–89 Christopher D'Arcangelo's action at the Louvre Museum, Paris, March 8, 1978. Christopher D'Arcangelo Papers; MSS 264. Courtesy of the Fales Library & Special Collections, New York University Libraries.

p. 97 Laurie Parsons, *troubled*, 1989. Mixed media, dimensions variable. Courtesy of the artist.

p. 100 Laurie Parsons, exhibition view of "The Spatial Drive: Security and Admissions Project," New Museum, New York, September 27, 1992–January 3, 1993. Photo: Fred Scruton. Courtesy of the artist and the New Museum, New York.

p. 105 Cady Noland at documenta-Halle, 1992. Photo: Klaus Baum. Courtesy of the photographer.

p. 114 Trisha Donnelly, *Hand that holds the desert down*, 2002. Silver gelatin print, 5 × 7 in. Courtesy of Casey Kaplan, New York.

p. 118 Trisha Donnelly, *Untitled*, 2014. Video still. Courtesy of Casey Kaplan, New York.

Martin Herbert
Tell Them I Said No

Published by Sternberg Press

Editor: Niamh Dunphy
Proofreading: Max Bach, Laura Preston
Design: Fraser Muggeridge studio
Printing: Tallinn Book Printers, Estonia

Cover illustration by Harrison King-Riches, made during a workshop led by Fraser Muggeridge at Camberwell College of Art, London.

ISBN 978-3-95679-200-7

First published 2016, first reprint 2019, second reprint 2025

Distributed by The MIT Press, Art Data, Les presses du réel, and Idea Books

Sternberg Press
71–75 Shelton Street
London WC2H 9JQ
www.sternberg-press.com